Guide to Financial Management in FE

Other Titles in the Essential FE Toolkit Series

Books for Lecturers

Teaching Adults – Amanda Hayes

Teaching the FE Curriculum – Mark Weyers

e-Learning in FE – John Whalley, Theresa Welch and Lee Williamson

FE Lecturer's Survival Guide – Angela Steward

FE Lecturer's Guide to Diversity and Inclusion – Anne-Marie Wright, Sue Colquhoun, Jane Speare and Tracey Partridge

How to Manage Stress in FE – Elizabeth Hartney

Guide to Teaching 14–19 – James Ogunleye

Ultimate FE Lecturer's Handbook – Ros Clow and Trevor Dawn

A to Z of Teaching in FE – Angela Steward

Getting the Buggers Motivated in FE – Susan Wallace

How to Teach in FE with a Hangover – Angela Steward

Books for Managers

Everything You Need to Know about FE Policy – Yvonne Hillier

Middle Management in FE – Ann Briggs

Managing Higher Education in Colleges – Gareth Parry, Anne Thompson and Penny Blackie

Survival Guide for College Managers and Leaders – David Collins

Guide to Leadership and Governance in FE – Adrian Perry

Guide to Financial Management in FE – Julian Gravatt

Guide to Race Equality – Beulah Ainley

Ultimate FE Leadership and Management Handbook – Jill Jameson and Ian McNay

A to Z for Every Manager in FE – Susan Wallace and Jonathan Gravells

Guide to VET – Christopher Winch and Terry Hyland

Guide to Financial Management in FE

Julian Gravatt

The Essential FE Toolkit Series

continuum

Continuum International Publishing Group

The Tower Building
11 York Road
SE1 7NX

80 Maiden Lane, Suite 704
New York
NY 10038

www.continuumbooks.com

British Library Cataloguing-in-Publication Data
A catalogue record for this book is available from the British Library.

ISBN: 978-0-8264-8805-3 (paperback)

Typeset by YHT Ltd, London
Printed and bound in Great Britain by Biddles Ltd, King's Lynn, Norfolk

Contents

Series foreword

THE ESSENTIAL FE TOOLKIT SERIES

Jill Jameson
Series Editor

In the autumn of 1974, a young woman newly arrived from Africa landed in Devon to embark on a new life in England. Having travelled halfway round the world, she still longed for sunny Zimbabwe. Not sure what career to follow, she took a part-time job teaching EFL to Finnish students. Having enjoyed this, she studied thereafter for a PGCE at the University of Nottingham in Ted Wragg's Education Department. After teaching in secondary schools, she returned to university in Cambridge, and, after graduating, took a job in the ILEA in 1984 in adult education. She loved it: there was something about adult education that woke her up, made her feel fully alive, newly aware of all the lifelong learning journeys being followed by so many students and staff around her. The adult community centre she worked in was a joyful place for diverse multi-ethnic communities. Everyone was cared for, including 90-year-olds in wheelchairs, toddlers in the crèche, ESOL refugees, city accountants in business suits and university level graphic design students. In her eyes, the centre was an educational ideal, a remarkable place in which, gradually, everyone was helped to learn to be who they wanted to be. This was the Chequer Centre, Finsbury, in London, the 'red house', as her daughter saw it, toddling in from the crèche. And so began the story of a long interest in further education that was to last for many years . . . why, if they did such good work for so many, were FE centres so under-funded and unrecognized, so under-appreciated?

It is with delight that, 32 years after the above story began, I write the Foreword to *The Essential FE Toolkit*, Continuum's new series of 24 books on further education (FE) for teachers and college leaders. The idea behind the *Toolkit* is to provide a

comprehensive guide to FE in a series of compact, readable
books. The suite of 24 individual books are gathered together
to provide the practitioner with an overall FE toolkit in specialist, fact-filled volumes designed to be easily accessible,
written by experts with significant knowledge and experience
in their individual fields. All of the authors have in-depth
understanding of further education. But 'Why is further education important? Why does it merit a whole series to be
written about it?' you may ask.

At the Association of Colleges Annual Conference in 2005, in
a humorous speech to college principals, John Brennan said that,
whereas in 1995 further education was a 'political backwater',
by 2005 it had become 'mainstream'. John recalled that since
1995 there had been '36 separate government or government-
sponsored reports or White Papers specifically devoted to the
post-16 sector'. In our recent regional research report (2006) for
the Learning and Skills Development Agency, my co-author
Yvonne Hillier and I noted that it was no longer 'raining policy'
in FE, as we had described earlier (Hillier and Jameson, 2003):
there is now a torrent of new initiatives. We thought in 2003
that an umbrella would suffice to protect you. We'd now
recommend buying a boat to navigate these choppy waters, as it
looks as if John Brennan's 'mainstream' FE, combined with a
tidal wave of government policies, will soon lead to a flood of
new interest in the sector, rather than end anytime soon.

There are good reasons for all this government attention on
further education. In 2004/2005, student numbers in LSC-
funded further education increased to 4.2 million, total college
income was around £6.1 billion, and the average college had
an annual turnover of £15 million. Further education has
rapidly increased in national significance regarding the need for
ever greater achievements in UK education and skills training
for millions of learners, providing qualifications and workforce
training to feed a UK national economy hungrily in competition with other OECD nations. The 120 recommendations of
the Foster Review (2005) therefore in the main encourage
colleges to focus their work on vocational skills, social inclusion
and achieving academic progress. This Series is here to consider
all three of these areas and more.

The Series is written for teaching practitioners, leaders and managers in the 572 FE/LSC-funded institutions in the UK, including FE colleges, adult education and sixth-form institutions, prison education departments, training and workforce development units, local education authorities and community agencies. The series is also written for PGCE/Cert Ed/City & Guilds Initial and continuing professional development (CPD) teacher trainees in universities in the UK, USA, Canada, Australia, New Zealand and beyond. It will also be of interest to staff in the 600 Jobcentre Plus providers in the UK and to many private training organizations. All may find this series of use and interest in learning about FE educational practice in the 24 different areas of these specialist books from experts in the field.

Our use of this somewhat fuzzy term 'practitioners' includes staff in the FE/LSC-funded sector who engage in professional practice in governance, leadership, management, teaching, training, financial and administration services, student support services, ICT and MIS technical support, librarianship, learning resources, marketing, research and development, nursery and crèche services, community and business support, transport and estates management. It is also intended to include staff in a host of other FE services including work-related training, catering, outreach and specialist health, diagnostic additional learning support, pastoral and religious support for students. Updating staff in professional practice is critically important at a time of such continuing radical policy-driven change, and we are pleased to contribute to this nationally and internationally.

We are also privileged to have an exceptional range of authors writing for the Series. Many of our Series authors are renowned for their work in further education, having worked in the sector for 30 years or more. Some have received OBE or CBE honours, professorships, fellowships and awards for contributions they have made to further education. All have demonstrated a commitment to FE that makes their books come alive with a kind of wise guidance for the reader. Sometimes this is tinged with world-weariness, sometimes with sympathy, humour or excitement. Sometimes the books are just plain clever or a fascinating read, to guide practitioners of the future who will read these works. Together, the books make up a considerable portfolio of assets for you to take with you through your journeys in further education. We hope the experience of reading the books will be interesting, instructive and pleasurable and that experience gained from them will last, renewed, for many seasons.

It has been wonderful to work with all of the authors and with Continuum's UK Education Publisher, Alexandra Webster, on this Series. The exhilarating opportunity of developing such a comprehensive toolkit of books probably comes once in a lifetime, if at all. I am privileged to have had this rare opportunity, and I thank the publishers, authors and other contributors to the series for making these books come to life with their fantastic contributions to FE.

Dr Jill Jameson
Series Editor
March, 2006

Series introduction

Guide to Financial Management in FE

There are around 400 further education (FE) and sixth-form colleges in the UK, plus a wide range of other Learning and Skills Council-funded institutions (e.g. adult education, prison education, work-based training organizations), which together spend around £11 billion or so of taxpayers' money educating around 4 million learners and employing 250,000 staff. As an example of the vast amount of activity that this generates, we could cite that multiple awarding bodies produce between them around 4,000 and 5,000 vocational qualifications. Complex record-keeping and auditing procedures in FE are carried out on a daily basis to enrol, maintain, monitor, track and progress the learning and achievements of this, the largest body of students in the UK education system.

These are large, impressive figures involving huge amounts of public funding. Because so much hangs on the efficient management of finance in the FE system, and it can be the gateway to institutional survival (or not), it is vitally important that all those who are leaders, managers, teachers and administrators understand FE financial regulations and processes. These include funding procedures, criteria for funding and systems for tracking and auditing learners.

Yet far too few people really have an expert and fluent understanding of the way the unfathomably scary function called 'Finance' actually works in FE. From my 14 or so years of working in senior management in FE, adult and sixth-form education, I recall that, at the mere breath of the word 'finance', some staff would recoil and run, slipping away into their specialist interests, as if to say, 'finance is not for the likes of me'. Those were the 'good old days', when fuzziness about finance was sometimes indulged with staff development sessions to inform the unrepentantly financially ignorant. Nowadays there is little time for such indulgence. There is an expectation that anyone in a management role in the learning and skills sector will be familiar with the financial systems through which institutions function, despite the complexity of these. Many staff therefore need help to cope with financial allocations and procedures.

To all those who need help understanding finances in FE, Julian Gravatt's book comes as a breath of fresh air. Written in Julian's inimitable, accessible and humorous style, this *Guide to Financial Management in FE* contains all you need to know to cope with institutional finances. Julian explains the overview of FE finances, including the background history of the various funding councils, the overall allocations to institutional budgets, the way these are made up, how auditing and financial procedures work and the various kinds of people and systems involved in college finances and auditing procedures. At a time when the Foster Review (2005), the government White Paper on FE (2006) and the Leitch review of skills (2006) call for widespread rapid improvements across the FE sector, this book provides an excellent handbook on finances for management staff. If you feel you need to know more about FE finances from a straightforward, useful information source, this book is essential reading for you. I thoroughly recommend that you read this excellent guide to finance in FE.

Dr Jill Jameson

Introduction

What this book is about

The aim of this book is to demystify finance in colleges. Too few people working in colleges understand where the money comes from. Too few people involved know where and how it is spent. Although the system for funding colleges is notoriously complicated, there are simple ways to understand how things work. This book will show you how.

The book will provide an overview of the major issues and trends in the college sector. It offers some practical tips on how to hold your own in discussions on college budgets. It helps readers understand the complicated ways in which colleges obtain their money and the simple ways in which they spend it. It looks at the various techniques used to manage finance in colleges. It covers some topical issues, for example the growing concerns about pensions or the growing numbers of college building projects. It links all of the above to the practical business of running courses.

It is worth adding that there are some things that this book doesn't cover. Because events move so quickly, this book isn't a commentary on this year's budget settlement for colleges or the latest twist of government policy. Nor is it a general finance textbook for the complete beginner. The book starts with an assumption that the reader knows a little bit about colleges and a little bit about finance, but not necessarily very much about either.

Chapter 1 looks at the general trends in the college sector and explores some of the financial implications. Chapter 2 explains how colleges manage their finances and the role of finance staff and systems in college life. Chapters 3 and 4 look at the income that colleges earn from government and other sources. Chapter 5 considers the important issues in how they spend this money. Chapter 6 considers the trends in capital spending, buildings and IT. Chapter 7 looks at risks, regulation and audit. Chapter 8 gives some tips about how to work out what is going on with a college's finances. Chapter 9 wraps up. The Notes section at the back of the book contains relevant background information and data on a chapter-by-chapter basis.

I cannot guarantee that you will become a finance expert from this one book, but I hope that you will end it feeling better informed about the way in which colleges manage their money, the key trends and the environment within which they operate.

1 The business of colleges

A good starting point for understanding college finance is to understand the environment in which colleges operate. This chapter looks at the size of colleges, their sources of income, the main areas of activity, their expenditure and the competition.

Size of budget

Between them, colleges in England spend £6 billion a year on their activities. Colleges are relatively invisible in the mainstream media or national politics yet account for 0.5 per cent of Gross Domestic Product. In other words, £1 in every £200 spent in the economy is spent in and by colleges.

Further education colleges in England

- A category that includes general and specialist further education colleges and sixth-form colleges.
- Main activity of colleges is academic and vocational education for students aged over 16 – including 650,000 16 to 18 year olds and 3 million adults.
- Colleges were incorporated under the 1992 Further and Higher Education Act (see Chapter 2).

There are now 378 colleges in England, including 99 sixth-form colleges. The average college spends £16 million a year and is often one of the largest employers in its town or suburb. The average college employs 640 staff, the majority of whom are part-time. There is, of course, no such thing as an average college but the scale of activities behind any college walls often surprises visitors. The largest college in England, Cornwall College, spent £68 million in 2004–5 and has 45,000 students spread across its seven main sites and numerous out-centres.

Although they are substantial education institutions, colleges are less visible than universities and schools. The university sector in England is much larger than the college sector in financial terms – £16 billion versus £6 billion. The average university is also larger, at about £100 million. Universities are therefore much bigger institutions locally and their presence is also felt locally through the thousands of students, many of whom leave home to study. Schools, by contrast, are smaller but much more local. The average primary school has a budget of less than £1 million but serves a much narrower community. The largest secondary school has a budget of £5 million but, even so, has a more substantial local presence.

Where the money comes from

The story in colleges over the last ten years has been one of growth and change. Total college income has increased from less than £4 billion in 1995 to more than £6 billion now (Figure 1.1).

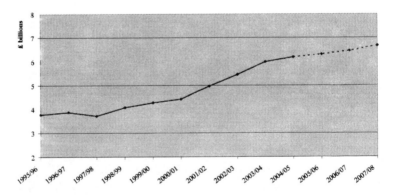

Figure 1.1 College income

Of total college income, 78 per cent comes from the government in the form of grants from the Learning and Skills

Council. This proportion has risen from less than 70 per cent ten years ago. Ten per cent comes from tuition fees and education contracts. The final 12 per cent comes from a variety of other sources. Overall, a 50 per cent increase in government funding over the last decade has made it possible for colleges to enrol more and different types of student.

The Learning and Skills Council

- Responsible for funding and planning further education in England.
- Responsibilities cover all publicly-funded education for over 16 year olds outside universities.
- Established in 2001, now has an £11 billion budget and employs more than 3,500 staff.

---

16 to 19 year olds – the core business for colleges

The main area of activity for colleges now is 16–19 education and training. In recent years, government policy has focused on encouraging more 16 year olds to stay in education and to improve standards once they are there. The UK compares badly against other developed countries in terms of the numbers of 17 year olds in formal education and training. Rising participation before the age of 18 also provides a base for expanding the numbers of university students. In 1998, the government set a target that 50 per cent of young people should have studied in higher education by the age of 30.

The role of further education colleges and sixth-form colleges in this expansion has been central. General, specialist and tertiary colleges account for 38 per cent of students aged 16 to 18; sixth-form colleges for another 12 per cent. The numbers of 16 to 18 year olds in education and training is at a twenty-year high and many of them are in colleges. The population of 16 to 18 year olds rose by 20 per cent in the ten years between 1995 and 2005. At the same time, the proportion in education and training has remained fairly static between 75 and 77 per cent. Government spending has risen to accommodate the resulting increase in numbers. Spending on further education rose by 48 per cent between 1997 and 2005. And spending on financial support has dramatically increased with the introduction of Education Maintenance Allowances for those who come from low income families.

Colleges have benefited from this expansion and now enrol on average 1,300 16 to 18-year-old learners. Colleges offer a large choice of courses for this age group, including A-levels, vocational alternatives and specialist courses. The government's curriculum reforms for 14 to 19 year olds take effect in 2008 and could create significant change in what and how colleges educate young people. The reforms will certainly have a high price attached.

The curriculum reforms are likely to bring some unresolved issues into sharp focus. There are overlaps between schools and colleges and intense competition in some areas to attract young people. The new diplomas are likely to require greater collaboration between institutions to give young people an adequate choice. At the same time, their introduction requires more joint working between local government and the Learning and Skills Council. Although the talk is of partnership, the competing agendas of different people and organizations in the 14 to 19 field make this particularly unstable. This government or the next could well initiate reforms

Adult learning and skills

Many colleges were set up to teach and train adults and this activity is what attracted many lecturers into the sector. Colleges account for the largest numbers of adult students, enrolling more than 3 million a year. The average further education college enrols almost 10,000 students a year, most on part-time courses. Participation by adults in learning rose in the first years of the decade, fuelled by demand for computing skills. This growth has now ended.

The government's ambitious skills strategy published in 2003 came with little extra money attached. As a result, the government's Learning and Skills Council (LSC) has had to redirect funds from other courses to fund expansion of priority courses. These include basic skills courses (called skills for life) in literacy and numeracy, and courses leading to level 2 qualifications. And as government funding has been targeted on these areas, a new policy has been introduced to expect higher fees from individuals and employers. The implications of this are explored in more detail in Chapter 4.

A focus on the needs of the economy

Vocational education and training has been the lifeblood of most further education colleges for decades. Sir Andrew Foster's review of further education in 2005 recognized this. He recommended that colleges should have a clear skills focus and that their purpose should be to meet economic needs. He made an exception for sixth-form colleges. This is now official government policy, through the FE White Paper, but the implications are still a little unclear.

The engagement of colleges with the needs of the economy has varied with external economic changes. Many day release courses for apprentices ended in the 1970s and 1980s because of de-industrialization, but colleges replaced them with training programmes for the unemployed. In the 1990s, this work proved more difficult for colleges because of the drive by Training and Enterprise Councils to reduce costs by using the cheapest provider – who often came from the private sector. There were regional differences. Colleges in the North East and North West retained a major presence in work-based learning at a time when London colleges lost much ground.

In the last few years, the reduction in unemployment and the expansion of government funding for apprenticeships has seen a different direction for colleges. Colleges were encouraged by the new Learning and Skills Council to use their refurbished buildings and skilled staff to develop services for employers. The LSC now contracts colleges for 35 per cent of its apprentices; other training providers subcontract further training to colleges, particularly in areas like construction. Forty-nine per cent of the contract value in the new work-based

Train to Gain programme went to colleges after a competitive bidding process.

Where the money goes

Although classified by the Office of National Statistics in the private sector, colleges behave like public sector organizations when it comes to their budgets. Most colleges operate on a break-even basis, with the sector as a whole managing an operating surplus of just 1 per cent of income. Sixty-three per cent of budgets are spent on staff; almost all the remainder on supplies and services. Colleges set aside 2 per cent of budgets for capital investment via an annual depreciation provision.

There have also been visible changes in the look and feel of colleges as a result of the largest building programme in the sector since the 1960s. In the space of ten years, more than half of the space used by colleges has been replaced or modernized. Taken together, colleges spend more than £700 million a year in this area and there are few principals working in old buildings who do not have modernization plans on their tables.

Cost pressures and trends

The fact that colleges spend so much of their budgets on pay creates a lot of internal pressure on their budgets. For the last ten years, price inflation has stayed at or around 2.5 per cent but annual pay increases have averaged 4 per cent in both the public and private sectors. School teacher pay has risen particularly strongly since the election of a Labour government in 1997. Colleges have struggled to keep up.

The cost pressures on colleges mean that pay absorbed some of the government spending that was directed to the sector after 1999. The efficiency squeeze in the mid-1990s forced colleges to increase annual teaching hours and to make redundancies. After 1999, government spending increased but some of the money was directed towards changing pay scales and improving the position of part-timers.

The pressure on college budgets has resulted in a rising share of expenditure on pay and a continuing need to find compensating efficiencies. If colleges do not keep their pay competitive, then they might find it difficult to retain and recruit staff. Research by the DfES in 2005 in staff recruitment and retention showed that staff turnover in colleges compared well with other sectors, but there is no room for complacency. Individual colleges report repeated problems in recruiting construction and basic skills lecturers and in finding assessors.

College size and character

The size and shape of the college sector has remained fairly consistent over the last decade. Several hundred independently governed colleges continue to coexist and compete, while covering limited geographical areas. To date, there have been no national mergers or other major change in the characteristics of colleges.

One consistent trend over the years has been the reduction in the number of colleges through merger. Forty years ago, there were more than 800 colleges. In 1993, there were 465. Fourteen years later, there are 378. In a twelve-year period, there have been 80 mergers of neighbouring institutions, some transfers to the higher education sector, a couple of closures and

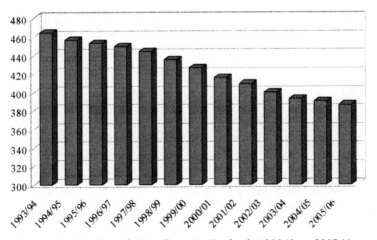

Figure 1.2 Number of FE colleges in England, 1992/3 to 2005/6
Source: LSC

two new sixth-form colleges. Consolidation has happened but the pace of change is slow compared with developments in the rest of the public and private sectors.

The low college merger rate comes despite many government efforts to encourage them. The Further Education Funding Council and the Learning and Skills Council both provided financial support to assist individual mergers, particularly in the period from 1997 to 2002. Merger has been an important tool to eliminate financial weakness in colleges. Local factors have also made a difference. There have been four mergers in Sussex in the last four years but only one in London. Some areas like Warwickshire have witnessed multiple mergers. By contrast, there have been no mergers in Cumbria and Gloucestershire.

The responsibility for weighing up the costs and benefits of merger rests with principals and governing bodies. The costs come early on. Mergers consume management time and as much as half a million pounds. They can easily upset staff and students. Governing bodies don't always agree who should be in the chair. Many merged colleges hit problems with enrolment in the first or second years. The benefits, on the other hand, come later and in the long term. Larger colleges find it easier to manage large building projects and to shuffle their courses around. A greater local presence can help the college negotiate with local partners. For general further education colleges, at least, size seems to correlate with better inspection grades – but it would be wrong to deduce from this that big is best. Smaller sixth-form colleges obtain excellent inspection grades and, anyway, inspection is not the only measure of quality.

Despite the predictions of some people at incorporation in 1993, the shape of the sector has not changed. Whether this continues to be the case in a period of tighter government funding and further reform, remains to be seen.

Competition

The college sector lacks clear boundaries to define its role. For every activity undertaken by colleges, you can find an alternative provider. School sixth forms, private training providers, Learndirect and universities all offer courses in the same areas that colleges do, although none of them covers quite the same range or does it quite the same way. This is not a new issue. A textbook on further education written in the late 1980s considered this issue and compared the college sector to eighteenth-century Poland. In some ways this is an unfortunate analogy because Poland was conquered by its three neighbours in the 1790s and divided up between them. Some of the gloomier principals think this could happen to colleges. In this scenario, the 2,800 secondary schools could expand their sixth-form provision – at present, only 1,700 of them have sixth forms and they cover a minority of the 16–18 age group. Universities could expand their adult access and sub-degree provision. Private training providers could expand to take on everything else, in particular the work for employers.

No future scenario should ever be ruled out but there is always reason for optimism. Colleges have proved in the last ten years that they can beat off many challenges and are now well placed for the future. They have economies of scale in A-levels which make them more cost-effective than school sixth forms, and vocational facilities that are unmatched by the private sector. The commitment of their staff, governors and students is a strong foundation for future development even if government policy and the external environment changes in a way that makes this more difficult.

2 Financial management in colleges

The first chapter summarized the competing pressures and trends affecting the finances of colleges. This chapter explains how colleges manage their money.

Legal framework

Colleges manage their money in a similar way to any organization in the public or private sector. Colleges have budgets, accounts, professional staff and finance systems. Financial management in colleges is governed by the same accounting standards that apply to UK companies and public sector bodies. There are, however, some important features which distinguish colleges from other organizations.

Incorporation

The college sector in England was created in a legal sense in 1992. Although many colleges can trace their history back to the nineteenth century, 1992 is a key year for the sector because this is when Parliament enacted the Further and Higher Education Act. This Act gave colleges legal form as further education corporations under the control of a board of governors. The process was known as 'incorporation' and also created a number of distinctive rules for colleges.

Incorporation

- Colleges were placed under the control of a further education corporation.
- The assets, liabilities and staff associated with the college were transferred from local government to each corporation.
- The governing body of the corporation was given legal responsibility for its future.

Governors are recruited from different groups (business, local authority, staff, students) and serve on a voluntary basis, without pay. The principal of a college is a governor. A model set of rules for how governing bodies must work is set out in Instruments and Articles of Government. These are equivalent to the Memorandum and Articles of Association for a company, but are standardized for all colleges.

The 1992 Act gave colleges the power to provide further education or services incidental to further education. They are not allowed in law to do anything else, though what this means in practice has never really been properly tested in the courts. The reality is that some colleges interpret the law widely to run a variety of business units from farms to training restaurants to job shops. This has the value of offering a broad curriculum to their students.

Another consequence of incorporation was formal confirmation that colleges have charitable status. They are not required to register with the Charities Commission but they are bound by the same rules as other charities. Specifically, governors have legal duties to protect the value of the college's assets and to act in the interests of the college rather than their own personal interests.

Incorporation created colleges as new organizations but also brought into place new rules for closing a college. The 1992 Act gave the Secretary of State for Education and Skills the legal power to close down a college ('dissolve the corporation') and transfer its activities to another college. As noted earlier, these powers have been used more than 70 times to implement mergers, but on only two occasions to close a college.

Many people who worked in the college sector interpreted incorporation as privatization. To justify this interpretation, they cited the removal of colleges from local authority control; the requirement that business governors form a majority of governing bodies; and the breakdown of the machinery for national pay negotiations. A new, aggressive College Employer's Forum (CEF), led by a self-publicizing chief executive, Roger Ward, devised a new contract for lecturers, which was fiercely resisted by the main trade union, the National Association for Teachers in Further and Higher Education (NATFHE). In the politically-charged atmosphere of the mid-1990s, further education was often cited as an example of privatization and the growing encroachment of unaccountable business-dominated quangos over the public services.

Now that more than ten years have passed since incorporation, it is clear that the position is more complex. Colleges were not so much privatized as nationalized. They are funded by a national government agency, are inspected by national organizations and are held accountable to national targets. For many purposes national government treats colleges like public sector organizations, but legally and constitutionally they are part of the private sector. They are classified by the Office of National Statistics as private sector organizations in the way that universities are. Crucially, this gives colleges the freedom to borrow money without it counting as public sector debt. The UK government has a target to keep total public sector debt below 40 per cent of Gross Domestic Product (GDP). Because they are classified as private sector organizations, colleges and university borrowings do not add to total public sector debt.

Government controls on college financial management

Colleges run their financial affairs like other private sector organizations of a similar size but they do so under a set of tight public sector rules. There are four specific areas where Learning and Skills Council rules place limits on college freedom over their finances:

- financial memorandum
- funding conditions
- audit code of practice
- accounting directions.

The financial memorandum is a device that is used in UK government to regulate publicly-funded organizations. Government departments use a financial memorandum to control the conduct of organizations as varied as museums, universities, and quangos such as the LSC. The LSC uses a standard financial memorandum to set some financial ground rules for colleges.

Financial memorandum

- An agreement between the LSC and college which sets financial standards in terms of accounts, audit and purchasing.
- Requires colleges to notify LSC of major changes in the college.
- Requires colleges to obtain approval for capital spending, borrowing and asset sales which are more than 5 per cent of income.

The funding conditions that the LSC imposes on colleges are set out in an annual funding agreement signed by both sides. This is like a contract and it places some specific requirements on a governing body. Since the mid-1990s, for example, colleges have been prohibited from charging fees to full-time students aged under 19. In 2002, this prohibition extended to all under 19 year olds, including those on part-time courses. Another important condition prevents colleges from cutting the volume of courses for students with learning difficulties and disabilities.

The central funding condition from the LSC is the rule that colleges must comply with annual funding guidance. This now runs to 127 pages and is supplemented by instructions in other circulars. The LSC is constantly inventing new rules in response to perceived or actual abuse and to focus its spending narrowly on the areas considered to be higher priority.

Funding conditions

- Colleges sign up to LSC funding conditions in their annual funding agreement.
- LSC requires full compliance with its annual funding guidance.
- Breach of funding conditions can result in request for repayment of money by LSC.

The audit code of practice applied by the LSC to the college sector sets out the audit rules. The code sets minimum standards for external and internal audit which are supervised by the LSC in financial visits often linked to inspections. Concerns about mismanagement of funds in a small number of colleges in the 1990s caused the audit code to be strengthened and auditors given a significant role in policing college behaviour. Like public companies, college governing bodies are now required to have audit committees.

The accounting directions issued by the LSC regulate the form and content of accounts. These directions supplement the accounting standards that apply to all colleges in the UK. Accounting standards ensure that organizations report their financial performance in a similar way, which makes comparisons and trend analysis easier. Without standards, businesses and other organizations could manipulate their accounts to boost profits and hide losses, to conceal risks and to enhance management performance and pay.

The financial set-up in colleges

College financial management takes place in a complicated and changing environment. The LSC is the main outside organization with an interest in a college's financial affairs, both as its principal regulator and as the provider of between 48 and 99 per cent of its annual income. Several organizations take an interest in college financial affairs. Some, like the Higher Education Funding Council, rely on LSC supervision; other grant-givers carry out their own financial monitoring. College finances are particularly closely monitored by any bank providing longer-term loans. As the debt taken on by colleges rises, banks will become more important stakeholders in college affairs. Loans are generally given on condition that certain covenants are met. Banks require security for their loan, which used to come in the form of an asset pledged against it, but which increasingly is delivered by promises to meet certain financial targets. Banks typically require colleges to make a certain level of surplus and to show that their incoming cash-flow can easily cover the interest and repayment bill.

A college's external stakeholders are important but the people with the legally responsibility for the college's financial health are the governing body. The standard Instruments and Articles place responsibility for a college's strategy and finances with the governing body. These responsibilities cannot be delegated.

Financial responsibilities of governors

- Determining the college's education character and mission.
- Approval of annual budget, safeguarding a college's assets and ensuring its solvency.
- Appointing and dismissing the principal, senior staff and clerk.

As a result, the core business of many governing body meetings relates to the financial performance and prospects of the college. Governing bodies often set up sub-committees to manage their financial affairs but are required to take the final decisions, for example on the annual budget. Although governors are unpaid, the prestige and interest associated with the role typically attracts several people with financial skills or experience, either from professional careers in accountancy or law or from managing businesses or large public sector budgets.

The ability of governors to supervise the finances of their college depends very largely on the competence of the staff they employ. The first and most important person in this respect is the principal, who has specific financial responsibilities in law and in the financial memorandum. The vast majority of college principals have teaching backgrounds (at least 95 per cent), but a few are former finance directors. The principal's role in ensuring strong financial management is part of their wider role in giving leadership to a college. This includes proposing strategies that are financially feasible, ensuring that resources are allocated in the right places and motivating and managing people to deliver the college's aims. Ensuring that there is a disciplined approach to financial transactions is just one of the contributions that a principal can make to effective financial management. But if the principal needs to fire the gun occasionally, the ammunition will come from the finance team, headed by a finance director or bursar.

Finance staff

The finance teams or departments that exist in colleges today are a legacy of incorporation. Before 1993, many colleges had delegated budgets and some freedom over financial matters, but none had full legal responsibility for their finances. Some colleges had large finance offices but, in a pre-computer age, this was often a sign of local government inefficiency rather than of the importance of the function. The role of finance staff was processing paperwork (payments and receipts) and supervising the budgets delegated from county hall.

This changed with incorporation, and at great speed. From almost zero, college governing bodies and principals found themselves with legal responsibility for multi-million pound budgets. The further education Funding Council at the time provided advice on what colleges needed to do to get ready and sent in consultants to every college to carry out a health-check. Top of the list was the appointment of a qualified accountant to a financial management position and, although this was not mandatory, there was a flood of new people into colleges around 1992. Many did not survive, but some have progressed to more senior positions. Many college finance directors are now vice principals or deputy principals.

The growth in importance of the chief financial role in colleges has been accompanied by the acquisition of new responsibilities. In many colleges, the person with the role of finance director is also responsible for other support functions like estates, IT and personnel. This is not a universal phenomenon. In some small colleges, an experienced accountant works part-time and has narrow finance responsibilities. In others, the finance director or manager reports via a vice principal with other responsibilities. But, as a general trend, the finance function has grown in importance. This reflects the growing risks associated with government funding, the expectations placed on colleges with large capital projects or new borrowing, and the need to pay higher salaries to attract individuals with the right skills.

The growing importance of the finance director has not been accompanied by an expansion of internal training or progression of finance staff. Relatively few finance people gain accountancy qualifications while working in colleges. Despite its size in financial terms, the college sector as a whole has very little presence in the three main accountancy bodies. This lack of training affects recruitment practices. There are many excellent finance managers working in colleges but relatively few promotions from lower level jobs to the top. When colleges have finance director vacancies, they generally advertise externally. Many finance directors switch from one college to another but there is also a steady inflow of people from similar roles outside the sector.

The role for finance staff at all levels has its challenges. Given their size, college finances can be quite complicated because of the byzantine way in which funding works. Expenditure is relatively straightforward apart from costs relating to capital projects and part-time teachers. Income, even though it comes mainly from a single source, rarely is. And the margins between income and expenditure leave little room for big errors.

Small errors are, unfortunately, a fact of life in colleges. The large numbers of students and the variable hours of part-time teachers make for a high volume of small transactions. Complicated rules make it easier to make mistakes. The lack of enthusiasm for paperwork can compound the problem. People rarely apply for lecturing jobs in colleges because they like financial discipline. Far from it. Some lecturers wish that colleges were refuges from the bureaucracy of life in the rest of the world and positively resent financial regulations and the like. This is not possible Learning and Skills Council funding and other programmes like Education Maintenance Allowances requires significant levels of internal discipline. Colleges are a long way short of banks in this respect but they have moved on a long way in ten years. Nevertheless, a finance job in a college can often be a challenge. Persuading an articulate academic of the need for this or that rule is not a task for the faint hearted.

On a more positive note, there is often a strong sense of purpose in colleges. Outside observers often criticize colleges for trying to do too many things and for lacking focus but this is only partly true. The people working in colleges generally have a sense that they are trying to make the world a slightly better place by educating and training students. Few people working in colleges are unaware of the buzz that comes with each new intake of students. Many people stick with finance jobs in colleges, despite all the difficulties, because they enjoy the upbeat atmosphere. There's some satisfaction in seeing your customers every day.

Finance systems

The finance systems in colleges were also transformed in the early 1990s, but this was more a product of the falling price of personal computers than anything else. The newly incorporated colleges bought finance systems off-the-shelf and installed PCs on finance desks at the same time. In the years since, the computers have been upgraded and there's probably a new finance system, but change has been relatively limited. The one-off savings from automating payment and accounting transactions cleared out some of the staff who peopled finance offices in the early 1990s, but there are technology savings still to come.

All college finance systems cover core processes relating to accounting, cash transactions and payments. Many also cover purchasing, debtors, asset management and costing. What is still missing is full adoption of electronic transactions to collect money and replace cash. Too many colleges still rely on cash transactions because this is a natural currency for low income students. The vast majority of adult students who pay fees do so in person because colleges have been slow to develop call centres or web enrolment. The bureaucracy associated with government funding is one problem because of requirements that enrolment forms are signed. The specialized nature of colleges creates other problems. The market for college software is limited. There are few rewards for companies to spend significant sums in improving finance systems.

The continuing fall in the price of technology and rising student expectations will prompt colleges to adopt better systems. The education maintenance allowance system introduced in 2004 requires more than half a million 16 and 17 year olds to open bank accounts to receive electronic payments from the government. This, plus prepay mobiles, Oyster cards and the like, is eliminating old obstacles to cashless transactions. At the same time, the growth of the commercial transactions on the internet will continue to raise expectations from students, parents and employers.

Budgets

The financial year in college runs from August to July and this is the timespan of college budgets. Budgets are set on a top down basis because of the centralized way in which colleges are funded and performance managed. College managers have to spend a long time negotiating key contracts but the information about expected income is relatively easy to gather from a few individuals. The budget setting process then concentrates on decisions taken about allocating staff. College effectiveness depends on staff working productively to develop, teach and administer courses. Because many of the costs relating to staff are centrally determined, through institution-wide pay systems, many colleges have systems to allocate staff time to courses and to academic departments. Given that most staff have permanent teaching contracts, the calculation of total hours makes it possible to work out how many hours of part-time teaching can be bought in. The central management task for heads of department is then to manage people effectively and productively – ensuring that lecturers teach their contracted hours and ensuring that necessary tasks are completed. And if budgets are allocated in terms of hours, good information is needed about the use and commitment of part-time teaching hours.

The complexity of controlling teaching hours prompts some colleges to go further in terms of delegation. Some colleges delegate responsibility for expenditure budgets, giving managers more freedom about who they employ for what purpose. This makes it easier to monitor the budget but more difficult to set. For example, difficult decisions need to be made about adjusting budgets to take account of a richer mix of more senior staff.

Decisions about budget delegation depend partly on the personalities of senior managers, but mainly on the size and scale of the college. Whereas a small sixth form college might run a highly centralized budget, a large, geographically dispersed college might delegate full budget responsibilities to departments or sites. In these cases, academic departments gain the benefit of any income or savings that they generate. This only works effectively in a tightly controlled environment where external funding rules are strictly observed. Setting delegated budgets in these circumstances is easier because simple rules about contribution can be applied. Where budgets are delegated, a college may require a department to contribute 40 per cent of its income to central costs, while leaving considerable freedom about how this contribution is delivered.

Whatever budget approach is taken, few colleges avoid the need to cross-subsidize between departments. Some degree of cross-subsidy is inevitable given that few colleges charge out central overheads. It is not always clear who makes the greatest use of central services like IT so cross-subsidies are likely to be taking place. More obvious are the overt cross-subsidies which occur where one department is clearly making a large contribution and others a much lower one. As colleges have a clear social mission, there is often a good case to support certain activities. But, if it is done too freely or without clear justification, the route to financial problems is a quick one.

The statutory accounts

Colleges prepare accounts in the same way as any other organization, public or private. A college's accounts provide useful information on its performance in the past and on its financial health. Colleges prepare their statutory accounts in line with the accounting standards set by the Accounting Standards Board (ASB), in particular with the Statement of Recommended Accounting Practice (SORP) for further and higher education. Colleges also take account of guidance contained within the accounts direction from the LSC.

Types of accounts

- Financial or statutory accounts, which are prepared for an external audience in line with accounting standards.
- Management accounts, which provide information for managers on a monthly basis.

College accounts are public documents and must be made available on request. Although the statutory accounts only summarize a college's activities, they contain useful information on its performance and prospects, for example on:

- any surplus of income over expenditure
- income sources, including the reliance on government funding
- trends between this year and last year
- the make-up of expenditure, including the cost of staff
- the level of cash balances and significant changes in either debtors or creditors
- the impact of any large capital transactions, for example purchase or sale of buildings and any new borrowing
- detailed information disclosed in the notes, for example on the number of staff.

A college's annual accounts are the tip of a larger iceberg of information that circulates within the organization. This information is accessible in monthly management accounts and, occasionally, from direct access to the college finance system. Accounting information is based on two sources:

- fact (payments, orders, sales, receipts, cash, etc.)
- judgements (asset values, debtors, liabilities, depreciation, etc.).

Accounting judgements have to comply with accounting standards if a set of accounts is to withstand scrutiny by external auditors. External auditors audit statutory accounts and give a formal opinion on the accounts, including:

- whether the accounts are 'true and fair'
- whether they are prepared in accordance with accounting standards
- whether they are extracted from accounting systems that are properly controlled.

If the auditor does not think this is so, they 'qualify' the accounts. Fewer than 2 per cent of colleges had qualified accounts in 2004–5, and these were generally on technical grounds. Auditors have a strong motivation to reach a correct judgement because they can be sued for negligence if accounts they sign as true and fair subsequently prove to be misleading. Sometimes such legal cases do not reach the courts because of settlements between the auditor and the wronged party. The external auditor of Bilston Community College paid an undisclosed seven figure settlement to the LSC over audits carried out in the mid-1990s.

Management accounts

Management accounts in colleges are prepared with different audiences in mind. Governors and senior managers require information on the whole college. Managers of individual budgets need to know how much they are spending and earning. The relevance and accuracy of the management accounts produced for these two audiences is a good sign of where the financial power lies within the organization.

Good quality management accounts are produced monthly, within days of the month end, include major commitments, are accessible to those who need them, and are easy to understand. Good quality management accounts ensure that there are no surprises at the year end and are a sign that the finance team is on top of its job in terms of knowing accurate facts and making reliable estimates. Accurate facts in finance systems require up-to-date transactions, correct coding of expenditure, prompt reconcilations with other data sources (for example bank records), and clearing of errors. Reliable estimates come from sensible profiling of budgets, systems to log commitments and close review of debtors.

Financial health

For ten years, colleges in England have analysed their financial performance using a simple grading system. Colleges in strong financial health have an 'A' grade while colleges in weak financial health have a 'C' grade. Those in the middle are grade 'B'. This system was introduced by the Further Education Funding Council and has been continued by the LSC. The grades are based on an analysis of college accounts and three-year financial forecasts, but are supplemented by judgement. The numerical calculation looks at college finances in terms of annual surpluses, cash balances, net assets and borrowing.

The financial health scores of individual colleges are rarely discussed or disclosed publicly, apart from in job adverts. You will often see adverts proclaiming that a college has 'grade A financial health' in an attempt to attract candidates. The trend in financial health scores is shown in Table 2.1. Increased government funding for colleges and tougher financial management improved the scores of many colleges between 1997/8 and 1999/2000 but there was a slipping back as a result of

Table 2.1 Trend in financial health scores

	1998	1999	2000	2001	2002	2003	2004
A	194	221	239	238	216	210	194
B	157	146	107	106	107	120	133
C	84	61	69	66	76	67	65

funding clawback in the years that followed. The LSC took concerted action in 2002/3 to improve college financial health by providing exceptional support to those in category C. A total of £38 million was spent in this way in spring 2003 on about 30 colleges.

The difficulty for the LSC is that it faces a moving target. Few colleges stay permanently in category C because they either take action to rectify their financial problems (for example by cutting expenditure or closing outcentres) or they are taken over. In the five years between 1999/2000 and 2004/5, at least 25 colleges with weak financial health (grade C) disappeared as a result of mergers. But, no sooner have some colleges improved their position than others experience decline, either because they miss key targets, make wrong decisions or take long-term actions with short-term costs. Colleges with large capital projects often slip a grade or two because of the impact of the large sums of money going through their books. The combination of low operating margins and high fixed costs makes it very difficult for every college to avoid problems.

The LSC is considering a significant change to the way in which it calculates financial health as part of its plans to introduce a Framework for Excellence. These plans would focus on three measures of financial well-being:

- solvency (the current ratio, which compares cash and short-term debts with short-term creditors)
- sustainability (the margin between income and expenditure)
- status (the net worth of the college, taking into account all assets and liabilities).

Whether these plans come to fruition or not, colleges will always need to be ranked and rated, in particular by the Learning and Skills Council and by the banks who lend them money. The banks who currently lend to colleges generally use the A,B,C rating. Judging the financial health of colleges will become even more important in the next few years because of the risks created by future changes in government funding. This is the subject of the next chapter.

3 Government funding

Importance of government funding

It is impossible to understand finance in colleges without some knowledge of government funds. There are two reasons for this: the size of the government budget and the conditions placed on the money allocated.

Colleges are highly dependent on income from the government via a single source, the Learning and Skills Council, and have become increasingly so in the last few years as the share of college income has risen from 69 to 78 per cent.

The change reflected increased government spending on further education and the falling away of alternative sources of funds, for example income from Europe and for training the unemployed. In part, this reflects conscious government decisions to route more and more money through the LSC.

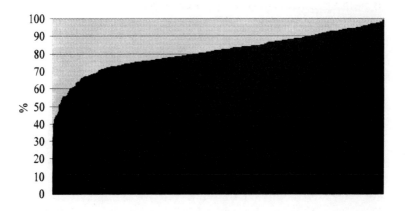

Figure 3.1 Percentage of college income from the Learning and Skills Council

The multiple conditions on government funding also have a massive impact on college affairs. The rules by which students can be funded have become increasingly tight. Between 2001 and 2005, a national system of funding audits forced colleges to improve their record-keeping or risk losing money. The rules by which colleges can claim funding have continually changed as have the rates at which each course is funded. These funding factors have forced decisions on which courses and qualifications colleges offer their students. Since 2004, the LSC has become more insistent that its money should be spent on qualifications that contribute to its own targets.

Taken together, the size of the government contribution and the conditions that are attached make government funding the number one issue in college finance.

Complexity

The systems used to fund English colleges are notorious for their complexity. For five years, the LSC in England has been grappling with the complexity of the funding systems it inherited from predecessor organizations. The LSC has made various attempts to simplify matters. When it was set up in 2001, it set out a plan to implement a single funding system for all colleges, schools and training providers by 2005. This came to nothing, partly because of other decisions to protect school sixth forms. It has proved difficult enough to introduce national systems for work-based learning and local authority adult education, without also taking on the added task of harmonizing these systems with further education.

Progress was made in some areas. The LSC did introduce a single national system for work-based learning in 2001–2. This replaced the 70 or so systems inherited from Training and Enterprise Councils and facilitated the introduction of a new drive to increase the number of apprenticeships. But every step forward in simplification was matched by a step back. A year after the new approach to work-based learning system took effect, the Treasury gave the LSC money to start employer training pilots. These involve a different form of work-based learning and were managed locally. The number of pilots and the money attached to them escalated between 2002 and 2006. In 2006, the government launched a new Train to Gain scheme with a single national set of rules. In the years that follow, steps will be taken to harmonize funding for Train to Gain and adult apprenticeships.

Although the LSC was a new organization, its inheritance of complicated funding systems gave it an initial reputation for bureaucracy. The LSC responded by appointing a bureaucracy task force, which, in 2002, recommended action to dramatically simplify the college funding system. The task force said that the LSC must move away from a data-driven relationship between the LSC and colleges towards a system based on trust. This work led to changes to the way that colleges were funded with effect from September 2004. They did nothing to harmonize different LSC systems. A year later, the LSC started an Agenda for Change to improve the way in which it worked and both the operation of the further education system as a whole. At this point, LSC staff estimated that they were running seven different funding systems and that the administration cost to the LSC alone amounted to £40 million.

Learning and Skills Council funding systems

- Further education, covering both 16 to 18 year olds and adults taking approved courses in colleges, universities and local authorities.
- School sixth-form courses for 16 to 18 year olds.
- Work-based learning, covering apprenticeships and related programmes in private training providers and colleges.
- The Train to Gain programme for adults with low skills in work.
- University for Industry/Learndirect programmes.
- Personal and community development learning for adults, generally routed via local authorities.
- Learning and skills for offenders, including prisoners and those serving community sentences.

There are various causes of the complexity of the systems used to fund colleges. A root cause is the continuing effort to make funding as fair as possible to ensure a consistent national standard of further education across a diverse sector and diverse country. Colleges offer a vast range of courses, qualifications and modes of delivery. There is much less standardization than there is in universities (where the predominant qualification is a degree offered to full-time students) or in schools (where every pupil has the same teaching hours). The complexity of the sector is a factor in determining the shape of the funding system, but it is not the only one. The ways in which local government funded colleges fifteen years ago were relatively simple.

A decade and a half of national government control added more and more conditions to the money given to colleges. The funding system has become a way to influence behaviour. Rewards and penalties have been built in to ensure that national targets are met. Frequent shifts in government policy mean that the targets keep changing. At the same time, funding bodies have added balancing factors to ensure that delivery of targets does not lead to undesirable consequences. For example, for more than ten years the LSC and its predecessors have placed a funding condition on colleges that insists that they must not cut the volume of courses for students with learning difficulties. Conditions like these have grown in number, as have the eligibility rules to prevent abuse. There have been times when a single transgression by a single college has resulted in the invention and application of a new rule for now and ever after.

The complex funding system for colleges is also a sign of sophistication. Information technology (IT) has revolutionized college management for good and ill. IT has made it possible for colleges to operate more efficiently and for information to be shared quickly and widely. IT has also made it possible for those who fund and regulate colleges to ask for much more information in return for their money. There is more and better data available to help the annual funding discussions between the LSC and colleges. It can be analysed in more ways to make funding decisions.

The LSC has regularly committed itself to simplification but change is difficult because of the impact of small changes. As well as being highly dependent on LSC income, colleges also operate on tight margins. The average gap between total income in a college and total expenditure is 1 per cent of income. Most college costs are fixed and spent on permanent staff. There is fine line between a college surplus and a deficit, and so in any one year, about 25 per cent of colleges do make deficits.

These financial facts produce a high degree of sensitivity to funding changes in the college sector. The LSC, in turn, takes great care in making changes. LSC staff model the impact of each change and try to find ways to compensate for adverse effects, for example by adjusting the rates paid or by introducing safety nets. The result is often to retain complexity in the system despite efforts to simplify.

Development of the college funding system

A good way to understand the systems used to fund colleges is to know how they have evolved in recent years.

Before incorporation in the early 1990s, colleges were part of local government. Local authorities controlled the finances of their colleges through control of staffing decisions, capital funding and, in many cases, control of the courses that were offered. Accountable to local electorates, it was logical for local authorities to link their grants to provision for local people. Under financial pressure in the 1980s, local authorities moved to delegated budgeting and linked their money to enrolments. An influential Audit Commission report, 'Obtaining Better Value from Further Education', published in 1985 encouraged more sophisticated approaches to budgeting and a few years later, central government required local authorities to apply delegated budgeting for colleges. This reform came in the 1988 Education Reform Act, which also transformed the funding of schools. Between 1988 and 1991, local authorities were required to introduce a budget formula that distributed money to colleges in line with their student numbers, calculated in terms of full-time equivalent students and weighted according to their course characteristics.

> **Funding formula under local management of colleges**
>
> $$£ = \text{WFTE} \times \text{Funding rate}$$
>
> where WFTE is the number of full-time equivalent students weighted by type of course taken.

Training and Enterprise Councils (TECs) were set up in the early 1990s and took a different approach to funding training for the unemployed and training of young workers. They moved away from purchasing places to purchasing outputs (qualifications and, increasingly, sustainable jobs). For a few years, as much as 75 per cent of the payment for a training place was conditional on a successful output. The output element in funding was scaled back by the LSC in its national funding system for work-based learning but has remained an important element of programmes for the unemployed (for example the New Deal). Output-related funding has recently returned to LSC funding in its Train to Gain funding, with 50 per cent of payments being linked to successful completion.

The Further Education Funding Council (FEFC) was created in 1992 and took over responsibility for colleges from local government in 1993. The FEFC consulted widely on its funding method between the publication of 'Funding Learning' in 1992 and September 1994. FEFC enthusiasm for its new funding methodology was visible in the distribution of a short video on the subject to all colleges. The video starred the FEFC's chief executive and finance director, William Stubbs and Roger McClure. It is unlikely anyone has kept a copy. The new system that was finally introduced in 1994 eschewed purchasing outputs in favour of purchasing enrolments on qualification-bearing courses. The FEFC funding method evolved as the decade passed but its key innovation was the use of a new currency to measure college activity. Funding units were calculated for every student. A price list (the tariff) gave values in terms of units for student enrolments, for each term that they stayed on the course and for their final achievement. At the start, a typical student could earn a college 100 units.

The FEFC multiplied the number of units that a college expected to earn by the college's average level of funding (ALF) to calculate its total budget.

FEFC funding method

$$\mathcal{L} \;=\; \text{Total number of units} \;\times\; \text{ALF}$$

where ALF is the Average Level of Funding per

Units per student = $(E + OP + Ach + FR + AS) \times WP \times AC$

where E   = units for a student's initial entry (enrolment)
       OP = on programme units for attendance
     Ach = achievement units
      FR = fee remission units, compensation for nil fees
      AS = additional support units
     WP = widening participation factor, linked to postcode
      AC = area cost factor.

The FEFC developed its funding system and its funding formula as a way of achieving change by remote control – a market in which the FEFC published a price list in units, which colleges competed to deliver. The system depended on matching units to desirable outcomes, which did not always happen. The large numbers of qualifications meant that there were too many outcomes. The FEFC price list expanded from its original two pages and became increasingly complicated. The prices offered by the FEFC often did not match college costs, particularly where courses were franchised to employers and voluntary organizations. This created opportunities to profit at the government's expense. The system as a whole degenerated into a hunt for funding units, which, in some colleges, infected every member of staff. By 1997, there was an acrimonious dispute between the FEFC and Department for Education over funding. The number of units delivered by colleges had risen from 130 million in 1993 to 180 million and the government could not afford any more – even though the price paid per unit (the average level of funding) had fallen by 28 per cent. Franchising now accounted for 15 per cent of course delivery and a few well-publicized scandals – in Halton and Bilston Colleges – resulted in a major about-turn. Government spending restrictions forced the FEFC to freeze college budgets in 1997–8. A small growth budget became available in 1998–9 and was targeted on full-time 16 to 18 year olds. The money for growth increased in the following two years but resources were still being squeezed out of colleges by the assumption that they would make 1 per cent efficiency gains each year as well as by the process of convergence. The FEFC made a large number of changes to its funding method in its final two years, right up to its replacement by the LSC in 2001.

The remit of the LSC runs much wider than the FEFC or the TECs that it replaced but it has found it impossible to resist the pressure to tinker with its funding system. Although some things stay the same from year to year, there have been constant changes to the way in which money is distributed. This is particularly apparent in the mainstream college funding system. In 2002–3, there was an entirely new funding formula.

LSC funding formula

$£ = [(\text{NBR} \times D \times \text{SCF} \times \text{AC}) - \text{Fee} - \text{Ach}] + \text{AS}$

where NBR = national base rate for the qualification
        D   = disadvantage element, linked to postcodes
        SCF = specialist college factor
        AC   = area cost factor
        Fee = deduction for fee assumption (this has been calculated using historic factors since 2005–6)
        Ach = deduction where there is no achievement, also calculated using historic factors since 2005–6
        AS   = additional support.

In 2003–4 the values in the formula were revised by large amounts. In 2004–5 the LSC introduced plan-led funding, partly as a response to the Bureaucracy Task Force and also as a factor for performance-related funding. In 2005–6, a new more rigorous approach was taken to shift funding towards targets. Performance-related funding was abandoned. In 2006–7, various funding rules were changed to cut LSC spending and Train to Gain was launched. The changes continue in 2007–8. Colleges will get one year to raise success rates above minimum levels of performance or could lose the entire funding allocation for a curriculum area.

Future changes

It is difficult to see an end to changes in college funding. At the top of the system there are ambitious ministers who are impatient for change because they have limited time to make an impact. Below them, the officials in the Department and the LSC are under constant pressure to stretch budgets to deliver targets and to rectify anomalies in the system.

The latest manifesto for change came in the Further Education White Paper published in 2006. This promised a more coherent approach to 14–19 education and training, covering both schools and colleges. If this happens, it will close the long-standing funding gap between the sectors and make the partnerships required by the new 14–19 curriculum easier. Making it happen will depend on the government's willingness to ride out the complaints of the losers from the changes, many of whom could be schools. At the same time, the White Paper called for the system of adult funding to become demand-led. In 2007, the DfES and LSC explained what this would mean in a wide-ranging paper called 'Delivering World-Class Skills in a Demand-Led Era'. This describes a system in which government decides which courses it will fund but employers and individuals decide where to take them. As well as outlining plans for more competition, the paper also introduces a new funding formula.

Funding formula for 2008-9 and beyond

$£$ = (NFR $\star$ SLN $\star$ PF) + ALS

where NFR = National funding rate
     SLN = Standard learner number
     PF   = Provider factor
     ALS = Additional learner support

This will not be an easy set of reforms for the LSC because its budget is already creaking with current demand. Adding new demands from individuals and employers will require tight control of costs. The LSC will have to ration the courses it funds, which is not very 'demand-led'. For colleges, the White Paper creates the prospect of a competitive free-for-all in their adult funding at the same time as they perform the complicated juggling involved in 14–19 collaboration. Most colleges will survive these challenges; some won't.

Short-term funding expedients have become the order of the day. Bright ideas emerge in Whitehall and Westminster. Instructions go out from the Department of Education and Skills to Coventry to implement the latest policy. Hundreds of people are then employed by the LSC to convert the policy into rule books, funding formulae and codes for computer systems. Tens of thousands of hours are then spent in colleges learning the new rules. Finally, at the end of the line, there's a puzzled lecturer and a baffled student.

In some ways this system is very efficient in distributing a ten-figure budget, but there are few things worse than doing efficiently what should not be done at all. The way in which funding systems operate in further education represents a huge waste of time and money. The LSC is quite good at what it does but, even after restructuring, it still spends much more on administration per head of population than its counterparts in Scotland and Northern Ireland. Colleges also spend more on administration than they ought to, simply to track what is going on. Yet, even so, they are left with a profound uncertainty about funding changes. The risks associated with funding make colleges more reluctant to take risks elsewhere. For example in reaching out to new employers and learners. The short-term tinkering has very real costs.

The overall government budget

The systems used to fund colleges do not operate in a vacuum but are constrained by the overall further education budget. In the halcyon years of the Further Education Funding Council – between 1992/3 and 1996/7 – the budget grew, but not by much. The FEFC system was designed to stretch this budget by taking money from colleges considered to be well funded and by encouraging low-cost expansion. The FEFC system delivered expansion but also a race to the bottom, leaving bankrupt organizations, declining quality and postcode lotteries in its wake. For three years, from 1996/7 to 1999/2000, the FEFC budget was frozen. Its funding system continued to emphasize convergence of funding levels, with efforts being taken to reduce the levels of franchising.

A different approach to funding followed the growth in government spending from 1999/2000 to 2004/5. Successive Treasury spending reviews directed large budget increases to further education and to the LSC in particular. Education as a whole benefited from more money. Further education received extra money so that it could deal with a rising population of 16 to 18 year olds, broaden their curriculum, provide for a massive expansion in basic skills and improve pay levels. The LSC retained the core funding system it inherited from the FEFC but made considerable use of targeted funds to deliver these specific objectives. Change on this scale is difficult and many colleges and training providers did not deliver all that they promised. There was, for example, a large shortfall in performance on the new apprenticeship programme. This prompted LSC clawback of funds and meant that the LSC made large, unexpected surpluses on its budget in its first two years (2001–2 and 2002–3).

Action by the LSC to avoid a repeat included various measures to spend money faster. Unfortunately looser controls from the LSC coincided with a more effective response by colleges and training providers to the various targets they had been set. Together, these two developments produced unexpected pressures on the LSC budget in spring 2004 and almost resulted in a large overspend. For the second time in seven years the Department for Education was forced to find extra funds for further education. In this case the grant was £130 million to keep the 2004–5 budget in balance. Other measures were introduced to keep spending within budget. A small change in the timing of payments to colleges from March to April 2005 helped the LSC stay in surplus because of the unique way in which it accounts for funding.

The pressures on the LSC budget have intensified in the period since spring 2004. Colleges recruit more students than the government can afford to pay for. Schools are expanding sixth forms, with encouragement from government. More apprentices are staying on, resulting in higher costs for the LSC. Across further education, there is a shift towards higher-cost subjects like construction and towards students who are more disadvantaged, helped by Education Maintenance Allowances.

The total LSC budget has not increased sufficiently since 2004/5 to cope with these cost pressures. The government's 2004 Spending Review was not particularly generous to the LSC because schools, higher education and childcare took precedence. Almost nothing was provided for the government's ambitious new skills strategy. Instead, the LSC has funded this by switching money out of mainstream adult learning by cutting course funding and by insisting that fees must rise to bridge any gaps. The squeeze has been on since 2004–5 and could decimate adult learning in colleges if the new fees strategy does not work. More generally, the budget constraint on the LSC will override any other consideration in the design of its funding system. There were seven years of public spending growth on further education between 1999 and 2006. The seven years that follow will be very different.

Understanding the funding system

It is impossible to summarize all the rules and issues associated with the systems used to fund colleges. It is, however, possible to analyse changing funding systems using a simple set of nine questions. These are summarized below:

Which organizations?	Which courses?	Which students?
What prices?	What formula?	How allocated?
What contract?	What IT system?	How audited?

The common threads in all college funding systems are the rules that determine which organizations can receive money and for which students taking what courses. There needs to be a way to set prices (funding rates), for using a formula to calculate budgets and for allocating the total budget to the relevant organization with certain conditions. These conditions are set out in the contract between funding body and organization – typically called a funding agreement. Finally, there needs to be an IT system to keep the score and an audit method to double-check the calculations.

In the FEFC period, it is possible to say that the organization's funding system evolved into a complex beast with arbitrary rules on courses, a lengthening price list and constant changes to student eligibility rules. The requirements in terms of IT systems and audits created problems for the majority of colleges. However some elements of the system remained relatively simple. There was a simple list of institutions (colleges plus a few others), the basic funding formula was simple and the contract was a standard funding agreement (common to all colleges).

The LSC system has left many of the attributes of the FEFC system in place, with lots of changes in terms of detail, for example the prices paid and the formula used to calculated funding. The main innovation has been an increasingly sophisticated and prescriptive approach to allocations. This has helped the LSC meet its targets. It has also made it possible for the LSC to take a different approach in its contract with colleges and the subsequent audit. With the LSC funding a plan, there is no longer automatic clawback if delivery misses the target.

The next few years could see radical changes. The Leitch review published in December 2006 recommended changes to funding in order to create a demand-led system. More specific proposals were published by the Department for Education and LSC in 'Delivering World-Class Skills'. This envisages a new funding formula and different approaches to funding 16 to 19 year olds and adults. There will be moves towards a common funding system for 16 to 19 year olds, whether they be in college or school. Meanwhile, employers and individuals will be given more choice over where to use their public funding. These changes are due to take effect in 2008. In the longer term, the government remains committed to introducing learner accounts.

Tracing the impact of the funding machine onto courses

Colleges engage in an annual budget negotiation with the LSC, taking several months. The rules change each year but recently the process has involved judgements on college performances against a range of targets. There's a line-by-line assessment of the college's ability to fit their courses to the LSC priorities. Finally, there's numerical jiggery-pokery as LSC staff adjust individual budgets in a way that keeps total allocations within available resources.

The senior management in colleges then divides up the budget and the associated targets between different academic departments. The exact standards specified by the LSC need to be cascaded downwards. If the LSC has insisted on the achievement of full-level 2 qualifications and the college has agreed targets, the focus shifts to delivery. This reinforces the shift towards top-down planning of courses and is reinforced by internal systems to measure performance. Individual lecturers feel the force of the funding system in the requirements placed on them to deliver. Colleges manage their internal affairs in different ways but all find ways to set enrolment, retention and success rate targets. This is as important for funding performance as for inspections. Detailed and accurate records are needed to create audit trails to IT systems. The systems themselves must be geared up to calculate funding. Lecturers are no longer required to count up the funding units themselves, but the impact of the funding system is as pervasive as ever. It's a life's work to understand the policies, rules and systems that are used to fund colleges. Many people earn a living from nothing else. But the changing environment in which colleges operate means that new sources of income will become increasingly important. Colleges will need to find ways to earn fees and win contracts. This is the subject of the next chapter.

4 Fees, contracts and other income

Income from the Learning and Skills Council is central to college finances but it is not the only source of income for colleges with adult students. Income from fees, contracts and other sources support the development of a college's own priorities. Alternative sources of income create some financial flexibility.

Fee policy

Fees have always been part of college finances, since their earliest days in the nineteenth century, when mechanics institutes and technical colleges charged fees for their courses to individuals and their employers. The growth of government spending on education in the second half of the twentieth century and the increasing numbers of young people in colleges meant that fees became less important in the overall total budget. Changes in the economy caused large employers to cut staffing numbers and to redirect training budgets. Companies no longer sent hundreds of apprentices to colleges for day-release courses. By 1993, when colleges were incorporated, fee income represented less than 10 per cent of college income – an estimated £300 million out of a total of £3.3 billion.

Fees became even less important in the 1990s despite the rhetoric about setting colleges free and making them more responsive to demand from individuals and employers. In truth, market mechanisms were used to allocate money between colleges but the way in which the government funded colleges reduced the role of fees. From 1994, the Further Education Funding Council insisted that colleges cease charging fees to 16 to 18 year olds studying full-time and provided money to ensure that colleges did not need to charge fees to those on benefit. In the ten years between 1994 and 2004, the scope of fee concessions extended. Colleges do not charge fees to anyone under 18, to anyone on means-tested benefits or to anyone taking a basic skills course. In the English college sector as a whole, the majority of activity, measured by course hours, is free to the learner. The majority of individual students pay fees but the total income from fees has remained at £300 million – now 5 per cent of the total.

Who pays fees in colleges?

- 16 to 18 year olds do not pay fees.
- Adult students do not pay fees if they receive means-tested benefits or take literacy or numeracy courses.
- Adult students pay fees if they don't fall into the above categories, but often at a subsidized rate. In 2007–8, the LSC assumes that fees cover 37.5 per cent of course costs.

There is a new emphasis on fees as a source of college income because of the need to use available public funds on the government's priorities. Government ministers now say that colleges must raise more of their income in fees. This policy was included in the government's skills strategy published in 2003, but only became a central part of government policy in the further education White Paper in 2006.

Whereas in 2004 adult students were expected to pay 25 per cent of their course, by 2010 this should be 50 per cent. This is the policy set out in the White Paper, which, over a six year period, requires colleges to double fees. Average fee levels are due to increase from less than £1.50 an hour in the middle of the decade to almost £3 per hour by its end.

Ministers in a Labour government did not want colleges to start charging fees to sixth-formers and to those on benefit, but they did want colleges to re-examine all fee concessions. Many colleges have offered fee concessions to price-sensitive students, particularly those on low incomes. This new approach hits older students particularly hard. For many years, colleges have offered discounts to pensioners. Fee income targets from the LSC combined with age discrimination rules taking effect in 2006 mean that the majority of colleges no longer offer such discounts. It is no coincidence that the number of over 60-year-old students in colleges is in sharp decline.

The new approach to fees in colleges followed several years of debate about fees in universities. The Labour government's higher education reforms involve higher fees for degree-level students combined with a more generous package of loans, grants and bursaries. University students will be expected to pay up to £3,000 a year from 2006 onwards but they will not pay the fee until after they graduate. Higher student loans allow students to defer the fee and to cover living costs. Poorer students may also get grants and bursaries. These reforms were highly controversial in 2003. The government almost suffered a defeat in Parliament because of a rebellion by its own back-benchers. But having pushed the principle of fees in universities, government ministers were happier to push the same principle for colleges.

The difference between the fee policy for colleges and universities lies in how the money is used. Extra fee income in colleges is needed so that the government can cut its subsidy to fee-paying students and use the money for other things. Extra fee income in universities goes straight into university coffers to use on increasing pay and facilities, with something left over for student bursaries. The government maintains its subsidy to fee-paying university students because of a promise that top-up fees would provide extra income for universities. In addition, the government introduced a new package of financial support for poorer students.

By contrast, there is very little financial support for college students needing to pay fees and the extra income they contribute is being offset by a reduction in government spending. Between 2004 and 2010 the government expects to save about £500 million from adult learning funding on the assumption that fees will rise to cover the difference. Whether this assumption holds true or not will determine whether colleges continue to offer courses to a mixed student cohort or whether they confine themselves to those who are fully funded by government – sixth-formers and adults on benefit.

The nature of fees in colleges

Fee collection in colleges is a complicated and occasionally cumbersome process. Most colleges offer a varied programme of courses, each of different length and level. The price charged for each course generally varies and there are often discounts and concessions for particular groups or individuals. In some colleges the responsibility for income targets is devolved to the relevant teaching department or faculty. This creates further twists if this allows more discounts to be given in certain circumstances. In general, the course price list is bewildering in its length and variety but the increasing emphasis on fees in government policy means that more colleges are taking control of the process.

Fees are collected at enrolment. Because the costs of running courses are incurred up front, colleges generally require payment before the start of the course and rarely give refunds. Some colleges offer extended payment terms for more expensive courses, but this is exceptional. Colleges generally provide some help for hard-up students through their learner support funds.

There is a good economic case for colleges to take a hard line on fee payment. Most of the costs of a course are fixed, whether there is one student or twenty. The income, by contrast, rises in proportion to the number of students. This is worth explaining in more detail. Colleges have to spend money up front to put on a course, including paying the lecturer to teach, making a room available and completing the administration to get everything going. This money is committed if all students take up their course place or if they change their mind. The college doesn't save anything if the student decides to leave unless so many students leave that it is possible to close the class and redeploy the lecturer elsewhere. Too much generosity with refunds could create real financial problems. On the other hand, each extra student is worth the full amount of the fees that they bring with no additional costs.

The economic factors that apply to colleges – costs incurred up front whether there's one student or twenty – apply equally in other areas of life. Package holidays, long-distance coaches, trains and planes all face high fixed costs and uncertain income. In all these other areas, the response has been variable pricing. If you want to travel with Ryanair or National Express, you know that you can get a better price if you book early. The companies involved have sophisticated yield management systems which calculate the profit from every passenger. Prices are adjusted to ensure that every place is full but also to charge the maximum amount to those who have no other choice. People booking flights late or turning up to hotels on the day often pay significantly more than someone who booked the same service a week earlier. Because the rules of this particular game are well known there are few complaints from customers about the practice.

Variable pricing exists in colleges but in a much simpler form. Some colleges offer discounts for early enrolment. Others give 2-for-1 or 3-for-2 offers. Up to now, fees have only played a small role in generating income and therefore less attention has been paid to the technicalities of maximizing income. This may change in those colleges that want to stay in the adult learning business. They will need to change their internal systems and make greater use of websites. Colleges who do this will be able to limit the fees they charge to price-sensitive students.

Higher education fees

Higher education fees are one of the most significant areas of fee income for colleges because of the greater willingness of students and employers to pay for higher level courses. Colleges benefit from this because they account for 11 per cent of higher education students in England. There are about 30 colleges that have more than 500 full-time equivalent students, and ten with more than 1,000. Higher education fees brought in £100 million of income to colleges in 2004–5, a figure that will increase as a result of top-up fees.

Higher education fees in colleges are affected by the regulations introduced in the government's controversial 2003

Higher Education Act. This established an Office of Fair Access and stated that universities and colleges could not charge top-up fees if they did not have an approved access agreement. The access agreement commits the institution to taking action to widen participation and to recycle some of the additional income from fees back into bursaries. In the first round of fee-setting, for 2006–7, about 45 colleges applied for access agreements out of the 100 who were eligible to do so. At a time when almost every university decided to charge a fee of £3,000, colleges took different decisions. Some colleges charged £3,000; others charged between £3,000 and £1,200. The final group, who did not apply for access agreements, stuck with £1,200.

The rules on full-time higher education fees apply until 2009, at which point Parliament will review the 2003 Higher Education Act. The rules do not apply to part-time courses, which account for the bulk of college higher education provision.

Higher education funding

Fees are only part of total funding for higher education in colleges. About 200 colleges in England also run higher education courses funded by the Higher Education Funding Council (HEFCE). In many cases, this funding is routed via a university in a formal franchise agreement, but as many as 100 colleges obtain their funding directly. Colleges have taken a leading role in some of the new initiatives in higher education, for example Foundation Degrees, and have a significant stake in the sector, particularly in towns where there is no university.

The funding of higher education teaching is a simpler affair than the funding of further education but it has its own peculiarities. HEFCE ties its funding to full-time equivalent student numbers and it uses a formula to price each student. Funding is increased for courses in more expensive subjects, high-cost locations (such as London), and students identified as being disadvantaged. Supplements are available to account for the greater costs of part-time courses and Foundation Degrees. The total resource for each student is then adjusted by a fee assumption, which is being held at £1,200 even though actual fees for full-time students have risen.

The formula is used to calculate the standard resource for each student. This is used in allocating growth funds and is also used to adjust funding on the basis of activity. If a university or college recruits fewer students than is assumed, then it risks holdback of money if the difference works out at more than 5 per cent. However, if an institution recruits too many full-time students, then it risks a different penalty relating to a target called the Maximum Average Student Number (MASN). The MASN penalty has been in place for a decade and reflects the government's need to control public spending on grants and loans. In the early 1990s, the success of universities and the then polytechnics at recruiting full-time students resulted in a significant overspend on grants.

The colleges running higher education courses have to deal with both an entirely different set of rules to those applied by the LSC and also with different relationships. Because many colleges receive their higher education funding via a partner university, the actual income per student is often significantly below the HEFCE funding. Universities deduct between 5 per cent and 40 per cent for the management and the quality assurance of college-based courses. The situation is often not very transparent and the position of colleges is further complicated by the different ways in which data is collected.

The greatest barriers to college expansion in higher education are ones of status. Government ministers and officials, like members of the public, too often think of higher education as happening only in universities. The proposal in the further education and training bill to give validation powers to colleges is a welcome reform, but the impact will be limited. Universities have a well-protected status compared to other public services. They are treated like private sector organizations yet handed large government grants. They retain freedom to decide what to teach their students and do not face the sorts of pressures that colleges do to realign their courses to meet the needs of the economy. The funding system operated by HEFCE directs funds to existing institutions year after year. Although colleges can bid for money for additional student numbers, the money allocated is marginal to the whole budget. And even when colleges have been successful in winning money for new programmes, like Foundation Degrees, some have found it difficult to meet targets and have had to hand money back.

Financially, higher education is a significant area for some colleges, particularly those who class themselves as mixed economy institutions, but a subsidiary one for the whole sector. Colleges receive about £250 million a year in higher education funding and fees. The quality requirements associated with higher education courses make it difficult to translate this income generated into surpluses.

Overseas students

International activity offers opportunities for colleges to generate new sources of income. Many colleges advertise for overseas students on their websites and an increasing number take steps to actively recruit from abroad. There has been periodic interest from government in encouraging this, spurred by an initiative from the Prime Minister Tony Blair to increase exports from higher and further education. This initiative started in 1999 and was recently extended. Although colleges have an important role in this initiative, the main focus is inevitably in universities.

In financial terms, universities generate £1 billion in annual fee income and are in a position to capture additional funds because they offer a wider range of services on campus. They typically keep the students for several years, as they complete degree and postgraduate courses, and charge each student more than £10,000 a year. Finally, universities benefit from the contribution that overseas students make to their research profile, particularly in the sciences.

Colleges, by contrast, earn less than £100 million and charge less per student – often less than £4,000 a year. Colleges generally keep their overseas students for shorter periods of time, often because they are preparing them for access to university, either via A-levels or foundation courses. Nevertheless the entrepreneurial nature of many colleges means that overseas activities are a growing source of interest. A small

number are investing in collaborative ventures abroad. Many
have overseas partnerships.

Overseas activities are no Eldorado for a cash-strapped
English college. While there is undoubtedly good money made
by some colleges from international students, this income
comes after years of investment in travel, recruitment agents
and supporting students once they are here. The choices
available to students willing to travel mean that colleges will
have to offer high-quality courses with good access to university. And the income is highly volatile. Malaysia sent substantial numbers of international students to English colleges
until the East Asian economic crisis caused an immediate halt in
1998. China has been fertile territory more recently but a tough
line on student visas caused numbers in colleges to drop
between 2003 and 2006. Rising oil prices create new opportunities in the Middle East and Africa. Colleges need to be
nimble to survive in the international arena.

Grants and contracts

Over the years, colleges have picked up a wide range of grants
and contracts to support their work. They have operated a
series of different training programmes for those out of work,
stretching from Manpower Services Commission projects in
the 1980s to New Deal courses set up by the Labour government. Colleges have participated in urban regeneration initiatives from City Challenge to, New Deal for Communities.
Some colleges have used grants of hundreds of thousands of
pounds to buy equipment or refurbish buildings. Colleges in
disadvantaged areas have run large European Social Fund (ESF)
programmes, although, since 2001, the money has been routed
through the LSC. Specialist, land-based colleges have tapped
into funds for rural areas. Colleges have run Learndirect courses
under contract to the University for Industry and will play a
part in the new skills academies. A small minority of colleges
run education and training courses for offenders, including one,
City College Manchester, which earns £40 million a year from
contracts which span a geographical area from Northampton to
North Yorkshire.

The list of initiatives and programmes is never-ending and can provide an important income source to the entrepreneurial college in the right place at the right time. At their best, these programmes allow colleges to use their training expertise, staff and facilities to equip local people with skills and to participate in local regeneration. Colleges across the country have been at the heart of local economic development. A virtuous circle has been created in which government agencies invest in the college, the college uses the money to raise the confidence and skills of local people, and this, in turn, encourages inward investment by companies and others.

Financially, these public grants and contracts add hundreds of millions to college budgets and are a major source of revenue for certain institutions. The money does not come without its risks. Unlike the grant funding from the LSC and its predecessors, the money is generally time-limited because the agencies involved often have a short life. Grants are often allocated against tight specifications in terms of outputs. Failure to deliver these targets results in demands for repayment, something that hit a large number of colleges running European programmes in the 1990s.

The employment-based programmes focused on getting people back to work present particular challenges. The focus of many colleges on skills for employment does not necessarily place them in the best position to deliver programmes for the unemployed. Jobcentre Plus and its predecessors have an overwhelming focus on reducing the numbers on the unemployment register and will reward organizations that deliver these goals. They are not always prepared to fund the full costs of training programmes and have therefore switched funds away from colleges to training providers with a much more limited focus.

The volatility of income from grants and contracts makes this dangerous territory for colleges but nevertheless potentially valuable. College business development units have grown in response to this, often employing a distinct team of full-time and part-time staff to run courses for a variety of agencies. A key job role is that of assessor, prepared to go out into the workplace to train and assess individual skills. The business development function is likely to grow more in future. LSC funding is forcing colleges to do new things. The Train to Gain programme rewards colleges for fast turnaround of students and strong engagement with employers. The Train to Gain budget has risen fast and the approach used will extend to more and more of the LSC budget between now and 2010. At the same time, the pressure on colleges to generate more fee income will encourage more engagement with employers. In regulated sectors, like construction, care and security, colleges have taken a major role in training and assessing low skilled employees. Sometimes the money comes from government; increasingly colleges will need to find it from employers.

Other income

Colleges earn income from a variety of other sources, as befits a sector with significant land-holdings and skilled staff. Many colleges run catering operations, though some contract this out. A few own or manage student residences, particularly those with higher education and land-based students. Town-centre buildings provide some colleges with weekend car parking income. Some land-based colleges own golf courses or acres of land let out to farmers. More generally sports facilities can provide a steady source of income, if not much in the way of profit. Likewise, realistic work environments in hairdressing, travel, catering and motor vehicle repair generate some income in the attempt to provide the right experience for students.

The scale of activity is wide but not very deep. Colleges acquired their assets in 1993 and they were given what was necessary to run their courses. Some colleges in London and the South East acquired property which they have subsequently been able to sell for good money, but this was then reinvested in new buildings. No college has the sort of assets to match the older universities, which generate substantial income and profits from subsidiary activities like publishing or conferences. The main business of colleges remains teaching and training. How colleges spend their money to teach and support courses is the subject of the next chapter.

5 People, supplies and services

Colleges spend £99 out of every £100 they earn. This chapter explains how and why.

The importance of staff pay in college budgets

Despite all the predictions about the use of technology in learning, colleges employ large numbers of people to impart knowledge and skills to their students. An average of two-thirds of college spending is on staff pay costs (63 per cent in 2004/5). In addition, many of the services that a college buys involve the employment of further people on its premises, for example in cleaning, catering or security. Taking these people-related services into account, colleges spend as much as 75 per cent of their budget on people at work on their premises.

Pay is also important in college budgets because the costs are fixed in the short term. Colleges employ more part-time staff than full-timers, but spend far more on full-time staff. Although some members of staff work on contracts with one month's notice, three months is typical for teaching staff. The days when part-time staff could easily be laid off because course numbers were low are also over, because of employment protection given to part-time employees.

Teaching and lecturing staff often account for a large share of the college budget – in some cases more that 50 per cent. The effective leadership, management and motivation of teaching staff is therefore critical to financial health.

National negotiations over pay and conditions

At their simplest, college pay costs are a function of pay levels, tax, pensions and staff numbers.

Pay levels are set with an eye on the market but within a pay structure influenced by national negotiations with trade unions. Before incorporation, a joint committee of local government employers and unions determined pay and conditions. The rates and rules for lecturers were written down in the Silver Book. Incorporation ended these arrangements but did not end national negotiations. Sixth-form colleges went their own way in establishing national negotiations with trade unions. The hundred or so colleges have maintained a national set of pay and conditions which largely matches those in secondary schools, despite the funding gap between the two sectors.

Further education colleges, by contrast, are covered by national negotiations between their employer organization – the Association of Colleges (AoC) – and up to six national trade unions. Employment issues are beyond the scope of this book but the financial point is the impact of these negotiations on college budgets. Each year, the negotiations produce a recommended annual pay rise and other agreements on employment issues. In 2003, the negotiations recommended a new pay structure which harmonized different pay scales and which replaced automatic annual increments up the scale with increments based on performance. There were short-term costs for colleges in adopting this pay structure but the possibility of long-term benefits. Many colleges have adopted the recommended pay structure but the scale of implementation is a matter of contention between the AoC and trade unions. More generally, the whole issue of pay remains contested territory between management and unions. National negotiations ensure consistency between colleges and reduce industrial strife but do not eliminate difficult choices between pay and jobs. For some colleges, the cost of an annual pay rise for all staff can be redundancies.

One issue that is not addressed in the national negotiations is the number of annual teaching hours expected of lecturers. The Silver Book set a maximum limit of 756 hours for main grade lecturers, calculated as 21 hours per week over 36 weeks. The Book contained rules protecting many lecturers from this maximum. In the mid–1990s, the College Employers Forum (the AoC's predecessor) recommended a model contract for all new staff which prescribed a 900 hour maximum (25 hours per week), and which swept away the Silver Book rules in the interests of flexibility. The differences between these two contracts was the cause of much conflict in the 1990s, with many colleges withholding annual pay rises from lecturers who refused to shift to new contracts. These disputes were resolved locally at the point where government funding started to increase. This results in considerable variety between different colleges. Financially, though, the important issue is not the contract maximum but the productive use of time.

The use of benchmarking to control pay costs

Average pay levels and annual contact hours are key ratios in analysing staff costs but they only tell part of the story. It is also important, in financial terms, to know whether staff are working productively. Productivity in colleges implies large numbers of students per lecturer (high average class sizes) and efficient teaching (low annual student hours) while ensuring high student success rates. There is little published work on college efficiency and effectiveness in these terms but there is lots of activity within colleges to benchmark their performance on these measures.

Further education benchmarking in the 1990s used insights and formulae developed in the 1980s in a Department for Education efficiency drive. This drive – the Joint Efficiency Study – was set up in response to the recently created Audit Commission study in 1985, which identified large areas of wasted expenditure in further education ('Obtaining Better Value from Further Education'). The Joint Efficiency Study ('Managing Colleges Efficiently') had various outputs but one of them was that a few key ratios could be used to measure the internal effectiveness of colleges. These ratios were the average class size, average student hours, average lecturer hours and the staff–student ratio.

$$\text{Staff-student ratio (SSR)} = \frac{\text{Full-time equivalent (FTE) students}}{\text{Full-time equivalent (FTE) staff}}$$

$$\text{Average class size (ACS)} = \frac{\text{Student taught hours}}{\text{Lecturer class contact hours}}$$

$$\text{Average lecturer hours (ALH)} = \frac{\text{Lecturer class contact hours}}{\text{FTE lecturers} \times 36 \text{ weeks}}$$

$$\text{Average student hours (ASH)} = \frac{\text{Student taught hours}}{\text{FTE students} \times 36 \text{ weeks}}$$

These four ratios could be combined into a single formula:

$$\text{Staff-student ratio} = \frac{\text{Average class size} \times \text{Average lecturer hour}}{\text{Average student hour}}$$

In words, the prime measure of efficiency, the staff–student ratio, was a function of how large classes were, how many hours a week lecturers taught, and how many hours a week students studied.

One of the guides written in this era ('Managing Resources in Further Education' by the FE Staff College) started from a position that college managers could do little to increase lecturer teaching hours. Management efforts in many colleges to increase efficiency focused on increasing class sizes and changing the curriculum.

Government support for the Joint Efficiency approach resulted in a national data collection system for colleges (the Annual Monitoring Survey), which had limited impact because it had unreliable data. It took the legal and funding changes associated with incorporation in 1993 and a national funding system to produce a college response. The government's survey was dropped and into the gap stepped a consultant using the same ratios. Ben Johnson-Hill had made a living analysing costs in the declining textile industry, but now shifted his attention to colleges. The benchmarking service he developed has at its core the key SSR ratio. However, where the SSR is an efficiency indicator, measuring the inputs into the teaching and learning, Ben Johnson-Hill added new measures to reflect variables now under college management control, in particular funding units per student (a measure of income) and average lecturer pay (a measure of costs).

The new formula looked like this:

$$\text{Unit yield} = \frac{\text{Average lecturer hours} \times \text{Average class size} \times \text{Units per student hour}}{\text{Average pay per FTE staff}}$$

The message of this formula was that colleges needed to take action in four specific areas to improve their teaching efficiency. They needed to increase the number of hours that an average lecturer teaches, increase the average class size, maximize the funding units (income) earned per student hour and control how much the average lecturer is paid.

The resulting figure – the unit yield – measured the income earned from every £1 spent on lecturer pay. In other words, it was a measure of the efficiency of the teaching and learning process. The great attraction of this formula was that it used data that could easily be collected in colleges and that were possible to control. Furthermore, with as many as 200 colleges signed up to the service, there was the possibility of comparing an individual college's data with a relevant average. Ben Johnson-Hill made adjustments to ensure that colleges could compare their figures to colleges in the same geographical area and to exclude colleges achieving poor inspection grades. Furthermore, separate figures could be produced for each curriculum area.

Benchmarking is widely used by colleges but Mr Johnson-Hill has moved onto pastures new, after selling his consultancy to the Tribal Group for £3.3 million in 2001. The basic formula described above still applies to colleges, though it is now more meaningful to talk about income rather than units – about the income earned per student hour and the ratio of income to lecturer pay. The questions that follow from the formula remain pertinent in all cases where there is a need to manage and improve teaching efficiency:

- Can the income per student hour be increased? (For example by increasing fees per hour or holding fees constant but reducing hours.)
- Can the average class size be increased? (For example by recruiting a few extra students or closing smaller groups.)

- Can the percentage of class contact hours be increased? (For example by reducing non-contact time for full-timers or by using part-timers.)
- Can average pay be reduced? (For example by using a cheaper or less experienced mix of staff.)
- Can these measures be introduced without harming quality or student success rates?

Other measures to balance the teaching/learning budget may prove more effective (e.g. cutting overheads), but this key formula holds until technological innovation breaks one of the existing rules, for example by allowing one tutor to support hundreds of students via distance learning.

Recruitment, part-timers and staff development

One in 200 of the people with full-time employment contracts in England works in a college. Even more work part-time, though the exact number is difficult to determine because some part-timers work in more than one college. The total college workforce numbers more than 200,000 people and is ageing. The average (mean) age rose from the early 40s ten years ago to 45 now. A few years ago, a Department for Education and Skills' report, the *Post–16 Skills Dialogue*, forecast that colleges would need to recruit large numbers of new employees to cope with government targets and to replace the people who have retired or resigned. The report calculated that the numbers needed in universities and colleges each year would exceed the numbers needed in teaching or policing where there are national advertising campaigns, and that the demand would also be for degree-qualified people, who can often earn more elsewhere. Recent cuts to adult learning courses and the imminent decline in sixth-form student numbers in some parts of the North may cast doubt on the more confident forecasts about growth. Nevertheless, recruitment will remain a major challenge for the college sector.

Colleges have always recruited widely to meet future staffing demand. In vocational areas, a long-standing approach has been to use people first of all on part-time contracts and then to make these permanent. Many people work part-time in colleges because this is all that is on offer but, for a large number of people, flexible hours are attractive. The college sector will need to use part-time working to attract staff, but only if it offers them a good package – not just pay and reasonable employment conditions, but a pleasant working environment. The financial pressures on colleges make it difficult to keep everyone satisfied all the time but first-class leadership and management may be the ingredient that makes the biggest difference. Good financial management skills are necessarily a part of this.

One challenging issue for college budgets is the drive to raise teaching standards through training and development of staff. A Centre for Excellence in Leadership exists to improve management training, much of it directly paid for by colleges. New lecturers have to acquire teaching qualifications, again partly paid for by colleges. New initial teacher training qualifications have been introduced, which are more expensive to run than the old ones. Short-term funding is available but the longer-term costs will fall to colleges. Finally, the Further Education White Paper in 2006 introduced the expectation that all lecturers would engage in 30 hours of continuing professional development (CPD). As learning organizations, it is difficult for colleges to object to these changes: but with budgets barely breaking even, it is always tempting to cut the staff training budget.

Pensions – the timebomb in college accounts?

Pay costs in colleges do not just mean salaries. Pensions are increasingly significant. The college sector spent £3.9 billion on total pay costs in 2004–5, of which £600 million went on pension contributions from both employers and staff. The money is handed over to the Teacher Pension Agency (TPA) and to local government pension managers in return for promises about the future. It is a system that worked for most of the twentieth century. A lot rests on it continuing to work in the future. If nothing else, pensions must help many staff resist the temptations to leave colleges for higher paid jobs in the private sector. The pay may be better, but what about the pension?

The profile of pensions in colleges has been raised as a result of rising contributions and visible deficits. Contributions from colleges have risen in order to close deficits and deal with future liabilities. As people live longer, the reported liabilities continue to rise and result in schemes reporting deficits. Actuaries use these deficits to adjust contribution levels. Colleges now pay 14.1 per cent of salary towards teacher's pensions and an average of 13.5 per cent towards support staff pensions. The rates could increase further.

Pension schemes

Teachers pension scheme (TPA)
- Lecturers pay 6.4%
- College pays 14.1%

Local government pension scheme (LGPS)
- Support staff pay 6%
- College contributions vary from 5 to 23% with an average of 13.5%

College pension deficits have become visible because of the requirement in the FRS17 accounting standard that colleges record them in their accounts for the year 2005–6. The total college pension deficit will exceed £800 million, which works out at about £20,000 per current member of college support staff. At first glance, the FRS17 deficit makes some colleges look financially weak. It has been necessary for finance directors to make clear that these paper losses record a future problem, which poses no immediate threat to the solvency either of the college or to the payment of pensions. The local government scheme is backed by the financial strength of councils that own large numbers of assets and that have the ability to raise taxes. Because local councils cannot go bust, the funds do not need to subscribe to the Pension Protection Fund.

The problem for their employer – the college – is not only that the pension cost is rising but that governors and managers have almost no control of this budget. The division of deficits and costs between different colleges depends on luck, history and the mysteries of actuarial science. The colleges with the largest pensions bill may be paying for the golden retirement of some long-forgotten senior admin officer. They may equally be paying the price of a hidden blunder made by an unknown professional.

The pension deficit in college accounts relates to the minority of staff who cannot join the teachers' pension scheme. The teachers' scheme works in different ways and is backed by government funds rather than investments. The government's actuary calculates that the teacher's scheme has a £140 billion liability if the FRS17 assumptions are used. Fortunately for colleges, the responsibility for this deficit rests wholly with the government. No effort has been made to allocate the share to each employer.

Pensions issues make some governors very nervous. Recent legislation has made the directors of companies personally liable for the costs resulting from negligence in the area of pensions. College governors are covered by this legislation but have protections in fact and in law. No college has become insolvent in the decade since incorporation and, if they did, the Learning and Skills Act protects governors from legal consequences so long as they acted reasonably.

Pensions will remain contested territory in the years to come. Staff will have to pay more for Local government pensions from 2008. Membership of the public section schemes will make it harder for colleges to compete with private training providers who do offer membership to their staff. The closure of private sector schemes could make the continuation of public sector schemes anomalous but reforms will meet strong resistance from unions. Lack of action will store up problems for the future.

Support staff

Although teachers and lecturers are the main employment category in colleges, there are many other people on the payroll. Colleges manage a number of customer-facing services to a large day-time population of students. These services are incidental to the core college business of teaching and learning but often essential for effective delivery. Starting at the front door, these services include reception, security and all the activities associated with getting students on the right course. This includes the website manager and person on the telephone switchboard as well as the people who handle information, advice and enrolment.

Inside the college are staff providing on-course administration (including attendance, examinations and references) and those who advise and guide students. In the classroom, there may be additional technicians and assistants to help deliver specialized courses or to support students with learning difficulties or disabilities. All colleges have a library or learning centre. Somewhere in the building there is likely to be catering facilities and childcare. Meanwhile, outside, colleges may have a share of the transport business. One rural college spends as much as £1 million on home-to-college transport, most of which is covered from fares charged to students. In some colleges, including those with religious foundations, there is a chaplain.

Supplementing these customer-facing services are corporate activities necessary to keep the college functioning as an organization. The finance team was discussed in Chapter 2. Other teams cover personnel, IT and estates, though the level of staffing varies. In the very smallest college, the person responsible for personnel administration may double up as a secretary. Larger colleges scale up.

Total expenditure on support staff accounts for about £800 million, or £1 in every £8 spent in colleges. Several factors have caused this expenditure to grow in recent years. Colleges have enrolled more full-time students and more students with complex needs. They have expanded services in response to this and, in many cases, have been paid by government to do so. There was, for example, a large increase in college childcare provision at the start of the decade. Curriculum innovation has been another factor in the change. As colleges buy and use more IT equipment, they have employed more people to make use of it and, in some cases, created new facilitator roles to support or even supplant teachers. Finally, the growth in support staff numbers has been prompted by the growing awareness of risk and of the consequences of getting things wrong. Risks have appeared everywhere. The risk that auditors would find errors in funding claims and recommend clawback of funds caused colleges to employ more people to handle student records. The risk to student safety and to the college's assets has resulted in more security staff.

The years of growth in support staff numbers are now in the past. The search for budget cuts is likely to target support staff because of the need to preserve teaching quality and student satisfaction. The greatest risk to a principal's job in a college is an unsuccessful inspection. Better to spend money on teaching and cut support services. A number of colleges have taken the decision to reduce childcare provision on the grounds that it is loss-making and benefits too few students. New technology may continue to make inroads into staff numbers. There is the possibility of government initiatives to share services between colleges

The services that colleges buy in – from cleaners to lawyers

Colleges were separated from local government in 1993 and incorporated as independent organizations. At that time, there were 450 colleges in England. The new FEFC funding system involved a high degree of competition. The new approach to inspections involved high penalties in terms of reputation for failure. The clear message to college governing bodies and principals was to develop an independent management capacity.

Many colleges bought in some services from local government in 1993 but many of these arrangements broke down as a result of changing college needs, internal changes in local government and VAT. The problem created by VAT is that colleges have to pay 17.5 per cent tax on the services that they buy in but cannot pass on these costs to anyone else because education is exempt from the tax.

Despite this VAT cost, the range and complexity of college

responsibilities resulted in the growth of new supply markets. Companies specializing in particular activities can often deploy staff more efficiently and effectively than a single college can, particularly where the activity is marginal to the main business of the college. This is the case with activities like catering, cleaning or security but also applies where the skills are specialized and where the college cannot afford a full-time member of staff.

Over the last decade, active private sector markets have developed for a number of services to colleges. Professional advisors help principals and governing bodies with strategy, legal issues, audit and architecture of new buildings. A small number of insurance brokers and companies have cornered the college market, accounting for about 1 per cent of budgets. A slightly larger number of companies supply IT systems and software to colleges. The supply of temporary staff is a significant business, as is the supply of certain transactional services like payroll and marketing services.

Colleges have been buying some items for decades. Exam fees, teaching equipment, books and computers are all necessary to keep a college running and add significantly to its costs. The total college market is worth almost £1.5 billion, taking all supplies and services together. There has been a recent drive to improve the way in which colleges buy these items and services, with a series of better procurement initiatives. All colleges have financial regulations containing rules on buying, for example on the level at which quotes or tenders are required. The procurement programme encourages colleges to understand their supplier markets better, to work with other institutions to increase their buying power and to take action to ensure purchases offer best value. Better procurement involves clarifying staff responsibilities, taking advantage of consortia and using technology to cut processing costs.

Tax – giving money back to government

Tax is a hidden item in college budgets but an important one. Colleges spend almost all of their budget inside the UK and pay tax on most of their expenditure. The sums are large and it is tempting to net them off against government funding.

The largest item of tax expenditure is the employer contribution to National Insurance (NI). Colleges are staff-intensive organizations and pay more than £350 million in employers NI each year. Together with the employer contribution to pensions, this creates a 25 per cent on-cost on top of basic salary. Colleges pay employer's NI on all full-time staff and most part-timers but not on those providing services as self-employed contractors. HM Revenue and Customs have recently tightened rules to limit the categories of people who can claim self-employed status, and carry out audits of colleges just like other businesses.

The other big tax expenditure for colleges is VAT, which adds 17.5 per cent to the cost of most supplies and services. Some of the items that colleges buy are exempt from VAT (books, exam fees), but most expenditure is not and colleges pay more than £200 million a year in irrecoverable VAT. The rules surrounding VAT in colleges are complicated because there is an oppportunity to claim partial exemption on building and energy costs where the college activity is defined as non-business (i.e. involves no fee). Colleges generally have to employ a tax advisor to help with the partial exemption calculation and can find themselves challenged aggressively by HM Revenue and Customs. The most lucrative area for VAT savings is in the construction of new buildings. The rules here can be particularly perverse. There is no VAT to pay on a new building if its use is entirely non-business. HM Revenue and Customs scrutinize this issue closely, which means that college building design is partly influenced by the need to eliminate VAT risks. New buildings have been artificially split in two – with no connecting doors or walls – simply to show the taxman that the facilities used by sixth-formers are non-business and are separate from those occupied by fee-paying adults. The risks of getting this wrong can be a 17.5 per cent bill on a multi-million pound construction budget. The consequences of getting it right are some oddly designed buildings.

The bad news on two taxes in colleges is counterbalanced by better news in two other areas. Income tax is paid on pay and benefits but as there are not too many benefits, the tax calculations are not as complicated as they might be. Some college employees have company cars, private health cover and other benefits; the vast majority don't. For these reasons, income tax is a relatively simple affair in colleges but one that costs college employees at least £750 million out of their basic pay. Finally, charitable status means that colleges do not pay corporation tax. This saves colleges a few million because the sector as a whole makes modest profits. For a few colleges, the savings are large because charitable status protects the profits they make from selling land and buildings. This brings us the subject of the next chapter, investment in the facilities that make colleges work.

6 Investment, IT and buildings

Colleges use a lot of assets to run their courses and their business. This chapter explains why and examines key trends.

Assets needed to run a college

Colleges run their courses from more than 5,000 buildings and learning centres across England; their main buildings with large industry-standard facilities are major community assets. Smaller learning centres in remote locations are often one of the few accessible public services for over-16 learners. The college estate is an asset that has made it possible for the government to launch various curriculum reforms confident in the existence of facilities across the country that could support expansion.

College buildings are valued in their accounts at £5.5 billion, which means that the average college owns buildings worth £15 million. The sector as a whole has 7 million square metres of usable space – about 30,000 square metres per college. In the typical college, this space is shared out between several buildings, some new, some old.

Financially, the operation of the college estate is important. Colleges spend as much as 10 per cent of their annual income on running costs and the equivalent of a further 10 per cent on the annual capital budget. In 2004–5, £120 million was spent on premises staff (caretakers, security guards, etc.) and £350 million on supplies and services. Another £90 million was spent on catering and residences, which are fully covered by operating income. Annual capital expenditure was £700 million, compared to less than £400 million four years earlier.

For many years, there have been voices questioning the need for colleges to own as many buildings as they do. Adult education could and does take place in borrowed or rented premises, including schools, churches and community centres. Workplace training can take place on employer premises. Innovative teaching and learning methods do not require buildings if information technology suffices. Given all these trends, is it perverse for colleges to own so many buildings? And are colleges constructing learning palaces or white elephants that aren't really needed for their work?

This criticism deserves an answer because it is important to understand the nature and reasons for college investment. Colleges own and run their own buildings because they need classroom space of the right size and with the right facilities. It does not cost much more to have a class of 24 compared with a class of 12, but the income is likely to be twice as much. Colleges need rooms of the right size to support their operations. The sorts of rooms that can be rented on the open market are unlikely to fit a college's particular specifications or help it maximize its income.

There are other reasons why colleges need control over their space. Colleges need rooms with the right facilities and equipment to support specialist courses. Some students can practise on specialist equipment at work but colleges cannot rely on this. Colleges wanting to run courses in anything from construction to science often need customized space.

Colleges need this customized space at times that suit students, with flexibility to make changes when needed. Renting space from another organization may not provide the college with the flexibility it needs, unless it has an exclusive lease. College managers need to construct complicated timetables to match student availability, room availability and staff availability. Timetables for younger students at sixth-form level match a school day but with less class contact time and more time for personal study. Timetables for adults need to offer courses at times when the maximum number of people are able to study, which in turn depends on the characteristics of the group, working patterns and transport availability. There is a lot of inertia in the way timetables are constructed but this reflects the need to ensure viable groups and the difficult calculations involved in changing them. But the wider point is that colleges need customized space at times that suit their own timetables.

Colleges also need their rooms to be grouped together in ways that create coherent programmes for their students, especially those studying full-time. Although some courses can take place in a single room, many college courses require students to cover a variety of subjects, using different equipment for each one. Many courses require access to IT equipment. Any student in college for an extended period will want access to catering facilities. And finally, if a college wishes to use its staff productively and keep its students moving quickly from class to class, there is a need for effective circulation space and good access from staff work areas to student course areas.

These accommodation requirements means that a typical college has a suite of generally available classrooms; several specialist areas (art and design, catering, motor vehicle, construction, IT); common facilities for students (catering, learning centre, public counters for enrolment); and staff work areas. There is no such thing as a typical college course offer so the layout of the buildings is never the same, even when colleges are new. Colleges may offer the variety of a small department store but they never operate in standardized buildings. The buildings that colleges operate in determine the courses they can offer. College capital investment is driven by the need to change the space for courses, whether this is to construct new buildings or refurbish old ones. In the 1990s, colleges ripped out engineering equipment and replaced it with IT suites. In this decade, there has been investment by many colleges to create construction facilities.

Managing a successful estate

Colleges spend a lot of money on their buildings but the right physical environment can have a positive impact on the overall budget. The state of a college's facilities makes a strong impression. Impressive-looking buildings draw in new students. Well-designed buildings persuade them to stay and help them study. If this leads to higher success rates, then there is an immediate payback in terms of government funding.

Conversely, poor buildings have a negative impact on morale. Student satisfaction surveys often contain praise for individual teachers and complaints about one or more aspects of the buildings, ranging from noise to the state of the toilets. Students may not praise a good building but they will let a college know when things are not right. And people who are really dissatisfied will tell their friends and family, potentially negating the college expenditure on marketing.

Messages about poor buildings also find their way into inspection and other quality assurance reports. The right facilities matter for a good course. Inspectors pick up on building weaknesses and have even reduced grades for colleges because of these issues. Good inspections do not lead directly to healthy finances but they help. The LSC and other funding bodies like to invest in colleges with good inspection scores. Good publicity can also draw in students and help colleges recruit teaching staff. None of these impacts is quantifiable but it is enough to focus attention on managing improving the physical environment.

The management of college buildings and facilities is a challenging task involving a lot of people doing a wide variety of jobs. There will be a mixture of employed people and contractors, working from the early morning to the end of the day. This can make it more than usually difficult to control overtime and contract variations. Some colleges still have resident caretakers; many have sold the accommodation. Either way, there are costs involved in providing 24 hours a day, 7 days a week cover on a call-out basis. Arson and burglaries do not happen in office hours. Colleges are insured against both but need to take action to reduce their likelihood. During opening hours, services like cleaning, heating and building maintenance are invisible if they work well and visible if they do not.

The pressure on colleges to reduce costs will bear down on building and estate management. Colleges with large capital projects should have a way to make savings; the others will have to make do. Short-term savings in building maintenance can help budgets balance but create a risk of longer-term costs. Cutting spending on cleaning or security could result in expensive accidents. It may only prove possible to find savings where new technology (for example CCTV) makes a new approach possible. For those colleges with contracted-out services, re-tendering may offer opportunities to reduce costs but only if there is a competitive market. Cleaners and security guards might only be paid at minimum wage levels. If so, there may be few opportunities for savings.

The difficulty involved in finding savings in the premises budget will lead many colleges to reconsider the services they offer students. Some colleges will look at their course timetables again with a view to cutting opening hours. It may prove cheaper to shift a few classes and to close on one or more evening. This saves colleges the money involved in opening, running and heating the building The reduction in government funding for adult learning has prompted a number of colleges to take this action – the end of night school, to quote a *Times* front page headline from March 2006. Other changes will affect catering services. Some colleges subsidize their catering services in the belief that this is the right thing to do to support low income students and a positive atmosphere. Higher prices might result in few customers and therefore no more income. Nevertheless, higher prices and shorter opening hours might well be the consequence of the search for savings. Finally, there is the range of services offered by colleges. Libraries, learning centres, childcare and sports facilities all play an important role in college life but all consume space and money. As the pressure on budgets tightens, the range and availability of such services may come into question.

IT and systems

The information technology environment in colleges is complicated because it supports three competing and occasionally contradictory needs. College IT services support the full range of corporate systems. Teaching staff from different disciplines and with different needs use college software and networks. Students gain access to college systems in classrooms, workshops and learning centres. This complexity and the relatively small size of individual colleges has limited the opportunities for

colleges to contract out their entire IT service in the way that
has happened in other parts of the public and private sectors.
Colleges buy a large share of their IT supplies and services from
the private sector but some parts of the operation are invariably
managed in-house.

Colleges also tap into a number of national services run by
government and universities effectively run a number of
national services which cover colleges. The LSC collects,
validates and analyses data from colleges on students, finance
and staffing. The key system is the Individual Learner Record,
which will evolve over the next few years if the DfES and LSC
move ahead with plans for a Unique Learner Number. This
development could have a far-reaching impact on the way data
are collected and used in colleges. Another major national
service is the high speed high volume IT network provided by
the Joint Information Systems Committee (JISC), a university-
owned organization funded almost entirely by central
government.

The development of software for college systems creates
interesting issues. Most colleges contract out software development to a few firms (for example Capita, Tribal). User
groups help bring together colleges to improve service but the
way in which the market operates creates constraints on
effectiveness. The British Education Communication Tech-
nologies Association (BECTA) published a report on value for
money in school management information systems in 2005.
This diagnosed problems in the school market that are common
to colleges. The report pointed to the domination of the market
by a small number of companies and the high switching costs
for institutions. The companies are under limited pressure to
improve their systems apart from the regular upgrades made
necessary by frequent changes in government requirements and
underlying operating systems. These upgrades can be charged
for. Meanwhile there is little innovation, for example in
transforming administrative systems to take advantage of the
internet. There are moves by the DfES and LSC to improve the
way in which data are collected and handled within the college
sector. Work is under way to develop a Unique Learner
Number and an FE Information Standards Authority is being

established. These are important developments which could centralize control of data in the further education system. If so, there will be resistance. Governing bodies, principals and managers will not give up control of their data lightly.

In recent years, the use of IT has significantly increased in colleges. According to BECTA, the ratio of full-time equivalent students to computers fell from eight students per computer in 1999 to four per computer in 2003. This expansion was driven by the growth in the number of IT courses and was helped by a number of specific grants. The increase in the number of computers has slowed since 2003 but there is evidence that computers are now used more widely. Colleges run fewer distinct IT courses but now embed technology into other programmes. Although BECTA figures show that computers are only replaced on average every four years, the greater power of newer models makes more things possible. Lecturers are better able to use IT; students expect more of it. More information is available on college intranets for students. More use is made of whiteboards and digital cameras.

These technological advances in colleges fall some way short of the predictions ten years ago that learning through IT would replace classroom learning, but there is no room for complacency. The government-funded Learndirect service is now well established and is supported by an efficient system which integrates most aspects of course administration and assessment. Distance learning has not taken off in further education but it has an increasing presence in business schools and corporate training departments. The high development costs for distance learning programmes are a major barrier but, once developed, the costs are much less than for traditional courses. Colleges occupy enough niches to feel protected from major competition from this front in the short term. The long term is anyone's guess.

Major capital projects – principal's vanity or essential investment?

Overshadowing all other building and IT issues are the steps taken by colleges to transform their estates in the last decade and in the years to come.

When colleges were incorporated in 1993, the state of their buildings was far from adequate. A national survey commissioned by the Further Education Funding Council from Hunter and Partners reported that a significant part of the college estate was unsuitable, that 20 per cent of college buildings were unsafe and that available space was poorly used. The report costed necessary improvements at £800 million. The FEFC kick-started a capital programme that has been carried forward by colleges in the years that followed.

The main achievement of this programme has been the modernization or renewal of more than 55 per cent of college buildings. This modernization has allowed colleges to reduce their space usage by 15 per cent at a time when full-time student numbers have increased. At the same time, colleges have invested significant sums to make their buildings accessible to those with disabilities. In some cases colleges have embarked on wholesale redevelopment costing tens of millions of pounds. There are some landmark college buildings that play a major part in local regeneration.

On a smaller scale, colleges have used targeted government funds to renew and create work-related teaching facilities in colleges, for example as part of the Centres of Vocational Excellence initiative. Colleges have also undertaken large-scale investment in information technology to create a teaching resource built on 300,000 personal computers in colleges.

The transformation of the college estate has taken place at a time when participation, attendance, achievement and standards have all risen. Although it is difficult to prove a direct link, research commissioned by the LSC from PriceWaterhouseCoopers showed a positive correlation between capital investment and participation.

The college capital programme has also had financial successes. Although it is difficult to be precise about the figures, there is clear evidence that colleges have reduced running costs by moving to new buildings. Colleges have financed projects from their own resources and from loans because of the confidence that new buildings will be cheaper to run and will generate more income. The LSC has been rigorous in requiring colleges to eliminate unnecessary space, to limit building costs to around £1,000 per square metre and to drive running costs down to £30 per square metre. Projects have only been approved if they meet stringent investment appraisals. A number of colleges have used capital projects to improve their financial health by converting buildings into cash, by reducing costs and by generating more income. There is some evidence that running costs do not always fall as much as predicted in new buildings, because more is done to maintain and protect them. Nevertheless, the overall financial impact has been clearly positive.

The pace of capital investment has increased since the start of the decade. Increases in capital funding have played a role in this but colleges have also used accumulated reserves, sold land and taken out loans to secure new buildings fit for purpose. The increase in the number and size of projects has happened even with the change in LSC capital funding policy in 2003. This change reduced the average LSC grant to less than 30 per cent for a while and increased college borrowing. Before 2003, the LSC automatically gave 35 per cent capital grants to colleges that passed its various tests. From 2003, LSC grants varied with the resources available to an individual college. A crucial assumption is that colleges can afford to borrow up to 40 per cent of their annual income. This implies that they can afford to pay up to 4 per cent of annual income on interest and repayment charges. This funding policy has remained in place but the increasing size of projects has resulted in larger individual capital grants. Some of the large projects approved by the LSC in 2006 were financed with the help of 50 per cent capital grants as well as large loans. Total college borrowing doubled between 2002 and 2005 from £250 million to £500 million. It is expected to double again between 2005 and 2008, reaching £1 billion.

Although the capital project finance is important, the driving force behind most projects has been the character of the governing body and principal. Development only happens if pushed through by some determined individuals. Some jaundiced lecturers might put this down to the personality of the principal but this is not an adequate explanation. There are such clear gains for a college in building afresh that governors, principal and senior managers feel it worth spending the time making a project happen. A new building creates an opportunity to redesign a college's operations and to overcome some of the problems of existing buildings. Lack of time and funds limit what most colleges do but the chance to address the quality issues that concern students, staff and inspectors is too good an opportunity to miss.

Colleges have a good record in delivering building projects on time and within budget. Although colleges are governed by volunteers and led, in the most part, by principals with educational backgrounds, there has been no significant failure in delivering projects. Delays have occurred because of local authority planning issues or financial problems but, once started, buildings have been delivered on time and on budget. LSC processes have had a positive impact in ensuring that projects are only allowed to proceed if they are educationally and financially viable and deliverable. To a great extent, the new buildings constructed between the mid-1990s and mid-2000s have been a good advert for the college sector. Not excellent architecture, perhaps, but a great improvement on what they replaced.

Design-and-build has been the favoured way in which new colleges have been constructed. Although some college buildings have been constructed on a partnership basis with a private developer (for example developers have taken land in payment), there has only been one English college building funded under a Private Finance Initiative (PFI) contract. Between 1999 and 2003, any college contemplating a large project had to seriously examine PFI as a possibility but few private sector partners were interested. PFI involves the public sector leasing an asset from the private sector for upwards of 30 years. There needs to be a long-term public sector commitment and large private sector investment to make a PFI work. Hospitals or transport facilities appear to have the size and stability. Colleges don't have either.

Future trends

The LSC's hope is that colleges will complete the modernization programme by about 2014 while, at the same time, reconfiguring space to meet the new demands of the 14–19 curriculum and the higher expectations of employers and individuals. This will require the successful completion of major building projects in the pipeline and action to persuade those colleges who haven't yet modernized to do so. There may also be a need to change some of the buildings refurbished in the 1990s.

The LSC therefore has had great ambitions for the college capital programme but seeing it through to 2014 could prove difficult. Changes to government funding have made many governing bodies nervous about the debt they are expected to take on. The growth in government spending between 2000 and 2005 made it easier for colleges to enrol more students in their new buildings and to claim funding for them. Many of the projects approved by the LSC in 2003 and 2004 did not open until 2006, by which time the growth years had well and truly ended. This has caused the LSC and colleges to evaluate future projects more carefully to ensure that they pay their way. It will prove more difficult to pay the costs of the debt needed for new projects. Unless there are clear opportunities to grow 16 to 18 year old numbers, colleges will need realistic plans for higher fee income or running cost savings. Reductions in adult learning funding also imply a reconsideration of the space needed in future. Although it would be sensible for colleges to include room to grow, space costs money. More generally, the art of value engineering – stripping out unnecessary costs from a design – is alive and well in college capital projects.

A central issue with the level of borrowing taken on by colleges is the security they offer to lenders. Colleges typically pledge one of their buildings to their lender as security, but it is difficult to imagine a bank wanting to take ownership of a working college building in the case of default. The bank's priority is getting hold of the money it is owed. Would the LSC let a college's finances deteriorate so badly that they couldn't pay a loan instalment? Would the LSC be happy to let a bank take ownership of a college building in compensation? So far, the answer appears to have been 'no'. The circumstances surrounding college rescues are shrouded in mystery but it is safe to say that in ten years no college has become insolvent.

Instead, the LSC and its predecessor, the FEFC, has intervened with exceptional financial support. This can take the form of a grant (as in the £38 million paid out in 2003) or the suspension of a repayment back to the LSC. The money is conditional on a recovery plan, which often leads to radical action and, in many cases, to merger. As explained earlier, 25 colleges with weak financial health disappeared through merger between 1999 and 2004.

LSC intervention has given the banks confidence to increase their loans to colleges, despite the risks associated with low operating margins (1–2 per cent of income), high fixed costs and large capital projects. Competition between the banks has also caused them to cut the interest rate charged. But as financial pressure on the LSC budget increases, can the past be relied upon in the future? The LSC no longer has a budget for exceptional support. A tougher line is promised for colleges in financial difficulty. Which implies more redundancies and more mergers.

Financial management in colleges is now tough and robust enough to ride out many storms. But it is not impossible that the tough financial climate of the next few years could see a stand-off between the LSC and a bank over the fate of an individual college. If this happens, it will change the way the whole sector is viewed. The key to avoiding such an eventuality are good systems of risk management, effective regulation and strong audit. These three areas are covered in the next chapter.

7 Risk, regulation and audit

This chapter examines the risks that face colleges and the way these risks are managed by the colleges themselves, by external regulation and by audit.

Risk management

If one stops to think about it, colleges are vulnerable to any number of risks. Buildings could burn down or could close because of a terrorist incident in the neighbourhood. A serious accident on the premises could maim or even kill a student. A pandemic illness could force the college to close. Foot and mouth disease only harmed cattle but forced land-based colleges to close for months in 2001. Bird flu could have much wider effects.

Smaller-scale incidents could be damaging in different ways. A fight between groups of students might leave no one seriously hurt but might hurt a college's local reputation. The discovery that a lecturer had a criminal record, perhaps associated with child abuse, could be very damaging. A scandal involving the principal could resonate for weeks in the press.

There is no end to the risks that could damage a college. It is impossible to imagine all the things that could possibly go wrong or to forecast the future. It is, nevertheless, worth trying, because otherwise college managers will not take preventative action or obtain the right sort of insurance.

Risk management is the art of imagining disasters, assessing their probability and working out contingency plans. In recent years, a degree of science has been applied to risk management and it has become a financial issue. All organizations are required to explain their system of internal controls in their accounts. These include their system of risk management. Colleges are subject to the same requirements and are required to prepare risk management plans for scrutiny by governors and auditors. These plans are also required for major projects.

The science in risk management plans is simple. Organizations are required to identify all relevant risks which may make it difficult to deliver its strategy and then to score the risks by assessing the probability and impact. This makes it possible to identify the most significant risks and to consider the action needed in response. A guide on risk management for colleges published in 2001 even recommended the following formula be used to assess risks:

Risk score = Probability × (Finance + Reputation impact)

Insurance is then recommended for high impact risks where the probability is low and where a market exists, for example fire insurance. Colleges spend an average of 1 per cent of their income on insurance – £60 million or more. Significantly, some of the greatest risks facing a college are uninsurable, for example falling LSC funding. Insurance is useful but what colleges really need is effective governance and management. The art of risk management is knowing when to minimize unnecessary risks and when to take calculated ones.

Regulation – preventing anything ever going wrong

The government maintains a large regulatory structure to reduce the risks associated with the college sector. Colleges are subject to all the laws that apply to companies of a similar size. Consumer law and competition law, employment law, laws to eliminate discrimination, health and safety law, the laws applying to property owners: these laws all apply to colleges. On top of this legislation, there is a raft of sector-specific legislation and regulation.

College funding is tied to nationally approved and designed qualifications. The performance of their students in obtaining these qualifications is monitored and publicly reported. A powerful inspectorate, the Office for Standards in Education,

Children's Services and Skills (OFSTED), examines and reports on college quality. Other quality agencies cover particular areas of the curriculum (for example higher education) or qualifications. The inspection system has played a significant role in raising standards but at the cost of standardizing the way in which colleges do things. Remarkably, inspectors take little account of cost in assessing quality. Inspection reports praise high quality but don't add criticisms if this comes at too high a price. The recommendations that come with an inspection rarely propose spending less on an activity. The move by OFSTED towards lighter touch, shorter notice inspections in 2005 has had a positive impact in reducing college compliance costs.

Earlier chapters examined the way in which the LSC limits a college's freedom of action. The finance and audit rules are one part of this but perhaps the most significant is the sophisticated and prescriptive funding allocation system. LSC staff now examine a college's course portfolio in detail and set funding levels in order to persuade managers to make changes. The combination of a stretched LSC budget and demanding national targets has severely restricted the ability of colleges to meet local needs if these are different. In relation to colleges, the LSC has a role as planner, performance reviewer, regulator and provider of both revenue and capital funds.

The LSC has had a good track record in preventing and dealing with problems in colleges in a way that prevents them from escalating: but there are significant costs. Colleges spend hundreds of millions of pounds on administration, including expenditure on compliance with general and college-specific regulation. Less regulation could mean lower costs for colleges and savings in public expenditure. Treasury pressure for efficiency could force the further education system down this road.

The audit regime in colleges

Audit provides a further set of controls to prevent things from going wrong in colleges. The audit regime for colleges is similar to that for companies and public sector organizations, but with certain differences.

A college's external auditor has a specific duty to report on the regularity of expenditure – to confirm that funds provided by the LSC have been used for the purposes for which they were supplied. This duty has been implicit on external auditors since the mid–1990s. Since 2004–5, the external auditor has to make a specific report on regularity and in the first round there were very few qualified reports. Internal audit in colleges has to comply with minimum standards set out for government agencies. Very few colleges employ internal audit staff; almost all contract the service out. A similar list of firms carries out internal and external audits but accounting standards and LSC rules prevent the same firm having a dual appointment. The firms providing audit services to colleges include two of the big four (KPMG, PriceWaterhouseCoopers) but are generally drawn from second-tier firms.

Auditors had a growing role in the final years of the FEFC, which lacked staff to monitor what was going on in each college. The FEFC relied on remote controls, for example through its funding method, but found that its data collection systems were inadequate to properly track what was going on. The FEFC therefore turned to the auditors, who provided evidence from the ground and who could be asked to give an opinion on funding claims.

Between 2000–1 and 2003–4, the FEFC employed auditors to carry out funding audits in every college. These audits caused problems for a large number of colleges but, in the process, introduced rigour and discipline to the keeping of student records. Ultimately funding audits cost a lot of money and time, while demoralizing staff. The reforms initiated by the Bureaucracy Task Force ended funding audits in 2004–5 for all but 35 colleges whose systems were considered less reliable. The numbers have fallen further to less than 20 in 2006–7. Meanwhile, the LSC has introduced a new, smaller programme of learner existence and eligibility audits to review the controls in colleges on these two issues.

As the years have passed, controls in colleges have strengthened and the level of external audit has diminished. This could be a temporary phase. The likely reduction in staff numbers in the LSC and the return of demand-led funding may necessitate an increase again. Although the LSC now has more sophisticated data collection systems, there may still be a need to check the evidence held by colleges. The role of auditors has expanded in other areas of the economy in response to the financial failures and scandal at Enron, an American company. US rules, which apply to UK companies with operations over there, require a very detailed check of internal controls as part of the audit. These requirements have not yet spilled over into colleges – but never underestimate the likelihood of more audit.

8 The college manager's finance toolkit

It is not difficult to understanding the financial position and prospects of an individual college but it is surprising how few people make the effort. This chapter gives some tips on finding information, analysing it and understanding the finance mindset in colleges.

Finding out things from the place you work

People are the best source of information about what is going on in organizations. A few finance directors or managers might be too busy or unapproachable. But do not assume this. People often like talking about their work, particularly if asked intelligent questions.

The annual accounts are another good source of information but are little used by college staff. College accounts are documents which must be supplied on request under the 1994 Charities Act. The Freedom of Information Act leaves little room for doubt that they must be supplied, even if this could cause embarrassment. Despite the public role of colleges, it is more difficult to get hold of accounts than it should be. Few colleges put their accounts on their website. The LSC collects accounts in its routine monitoring and puts some of the data on its own website. It falls a long way short the Charity Commission, whose register of charities increasingly provides on-line access to a scanned copy of the financial statements of charities.

A third good source of information are the management accounts and budget reports circulated within a college. Some of these reports can be too detailed but if there is summary information available for governors this is always worth reading.

Governors are lay people and require information to be presented in a comprehensible form. Finance reports to governors are always worth reading, if you are interested.

How to look like you know what's going on

Getting hold of information is one thing. Being able to make use of it is another. The first step is being able to translate and explain the jargon. The second is to understand some of the basic rules in college finance. The following summarizes ten secrets for financial success.

Ten secrets for financial success in colleges

1. Understand the business that colleges are in. Their costs are fixed, their income is volatile and the financial gain from each extra student (the marginal benefit) is high. With costs being substantially fixed, a management priority is high utilization of staff and buildings through effective timetabling.

2. Nothing matters as much as cash flow. Cash coming in should exceed the cash going out, which requires, above all, a tight control of income to ensure that anyone who owes the college money (its debtors) are invoiced quickly and pay promptly.

3. Don't offer discounts or promises to reduce invoices (credit notes) if you don't have authority to do so.

4. Any new activity needs to generate income to cover its direct costs, plus a full contribution to overheads and towards the target surplus. Surpluses are necessary to generate cash reserves. These, in turn, are needed to cover unexpected losses and pay for capital expenditure.

5. Know the financial regulations and what they require in terms of handling income, recruiting staff, making purchases or handling budgets.

6. Calculate the full, whole-life costs of large purchases, taking account of service and maintenance expenditure. Don't forget VAT.

7. Keep a track of any equipment or assets that you are responsible for. If there's lots of it, ensure you have a system for doing so.

8. Plan the spending of any budget that you are responsible for and review this plan in the light of information in the official management accounts. Keep a track of commitments. Take action to correct significant errors in the accounts but not trivial miscodings.

9. Appreciate that colleges operate within a legal and financial framework that is common to all companies and public services. Colleges have no escape from the need to process financial transactions promptly and accurately, from the need to keep good accounting records, from the need to answer audit questions or from the need to pay tax.

10. Know the broad financial position of the place where you work. Your future employment could depend on this knowledge.

Understanding the role of finance

Finance is often an unpopular topic in colleges. College finance staff sometimes find themselves bringing bad news to their colleagues. Lecturers often dislike financial regulations, which fetter their creativity and remind some of them of the bureaucracy they escaped in the corporate world.

When budgets are tight, the role of finance simplifies into saying 'no'. No matter how good the idea or how likeable the proponent, the answer is 'no'. The inspectors may insist, the auditors may command, it may even be a health and safety priority. Doesn't matter. The job is to guard the budget and control the spending. If the finance person says no, their colleague may go away and find the money without their help. It may even be unnecessary. Occasionally, they say 'yes'. For the want of a fuse, the college could close. But most of the time, it's 'no'.

Finance is not, to tell the truth, a well-understood job in colleges. The popular image is of a bean counter, enjoying saying no so that he can close the door at the end of the day and count the money. The less spending, the better. The more control, the happier. Never mind the quality, feel the size of the surplus.

It's a good question whether colleges should be making surpluses at all. One school of thought says they shouldn't bother. Isn't a surplus simply money that should have been spent but wasn't? Don't students suffer if colleges hoard their cash? Don't all good organizations make deficits? It's a fair point. Football clubs do it. Theatres are notorious for it. Secondary schools often set deficit budgets.

Take a step back. There's a difference. Chelsea Football Club has a billionaire backer from Russia. Local authorities pay the bills for schools. Who bails out a college if it makes repeated deficits and runs out of cash? And at what cost in terms of giving up control?

Money in the bank is the first step to independence. Is there a point where a college has more than it needs? Definitely. Some charities have reserves that could last them for years if nothing else came in. The Charity Commission says that two years' worth of reserves is enough. Most colleges have much less. Their cash would last them three to six months. Increasingly, they'll need more to pay for long-term commitments like staff pensions and up-to-date facilities. If colleges want to survive to 2020, they need to build up reserves by making surpluses.

The way in which colleges earn their income creates great nervousness. College managers know they should be making surpluses but sometimes find deficits at the end of the year because of an unexpected turn of events. When there are significant funding changes, as in 2002–3, colleges spent most of the year in the dark over their performance. At the end of the year, some of them found they'd missed their targets – retrospectively and because of rules their staff failed to comprehend. Will this happen again when the funding changes in 2008–9?

Surpluses create confidence. Deficits and funding volatility create fear, uncertainty and doubt. Colleges have found that their greatest risk is government funding and that there is little that they can do to manage it. Inevitably, this induces caution, which can give finance staff a bad name.

The secret to strong college management is to create a culture in which sensible financial thinking is internalized by all managers. If this happens, the finance director no longer needs to say 'no' because his or her colleagues won't even ask if they don't need it. In these cases, the finance director can focus on what really matters in the college, which is the systems for measuring financial performance and the effective allocation of money to deliver the college's aims.

9 Conclusion

The importance of finance

In November 2005, Sir Andrew Foster published his report on further education, 'Realising the Potential'. Sir Andrew was commissioned by the then Secretary of State to carry out this review. The government made an official response to the report a few months later in the further education White Paper, 'Raising Standards, Improving Life Chances'.

The Foster Report is a landmark in further education but barely covers finance or financial issues. Although he is the former chief executive of the Audit Commission, Sir Andrew chose to focus on issues like the purpose of colleges, the structure of the sector and the need to energize staff. He commented on the gap between what colleges wanted to do, what they could do and what they are funded to do. He left it to others to work out how to close these gaps, perhaps by constructing a national learning model to match the economic models used by the Treasury. The Foster Report recommended new initiatives but did not cost them.

Financial issues deserved greater coverage in the Foster Report, just as they need more attention in college inspections. Finance is the language used to translate decisions into action. Budgets report the real priorities of an organization. The accounts keep the official score. The financial issues explored in this book – the cost pressures, the complexity of government funding, the difficulties associated with other sources of income – create very real challenges for colleges and explain some of their actions. The limits created by finance constrain the most ambitious and well-thought-out plan.

The problem with predictions

This book has examined the development of finance in colleges over recent years and identified some trends. Many of these trends will continue but with a significant warning: it is impossible to predict the future, particularly when changes come in unexpected directions.

Back in 1993, commentators predicted that incorporation would result in college closures and a growth in fee income from employers. No one foresaw the massive expansion of a few colleges on the back of public funds and the subsequent attempts of the Further Education Funding Council to control the system by expanding its rulebook.

No one in 1998 predicted the large increase in public spending on colleges over the next seven years or the fact that the extra money would be absorbed in the costs of extra students, in the costs of a broader, more work-related curriculum and in higher pay costs to deal with historic inequalities.

Meanwhile the confident predictions made at the same time about the explosive impact of the internet have not come to fruition. Mobiles, digital cameras and the World Wide Web have changed the way in which people work and learn in colleges but they have not, yet, changed the basic interaction between teacher and student.

Given these precedents, does anyone in 2007 appreciate the scale of the changes to follow or know which things will barely change at all?

Where college finance will go next

Despite the caveats there are some predictions that have more chance of realization.

To start with, it is safe to predict that government policy will remain in continual flux because of the demands of the 24-hour-news media and the political process. Major programmes like the 14–19 curriculum reforms will be subject to constant tinkering before they reach their expected fruition in 2013.

Another safe prediction is that public spending will remain tight and that this will prompt a search for greater efficiency. A contention of this book is that there is still no magic bullet to improve efficiency. The only proven ways to raise efficiency in colleges involve tackling pay levels, utilization, class sizes and overheads. This is messy and difficult work. The consequences for quality and success rates must be taken into account.

Increased competition between colleges and others is a safe bet. Colleges will compete with schools for the right to educate young people. The falling population and the likelihood that more young people will stay in education create a shifting market, particularly if curriculum changes shake up what is on offer. Colleges will compete with universities for higher skilled, sub-degree work. Colleges will compete with private providers for the right to offer government-funded training. This competition is likely to blur some of the boundaries between colleges and the private sector.

The shift towards greater competition in the public services is driven by long-standing UK government objectives. Since the 1980s and even before then, the UK government has taken a strong stance in favour of free trade, including free trade in services. This occasionally puts the UK at odds with the governments of other major economies but is a logical position for the government to adopt, given the importance of services to our economic health. The logic of this position leads to the UK government's stance to support more free trade in the public services and to open up more of them to competition. This position is likely to continue whoever is in power. The implication for colleges is that government will use market mechanisms to foster competition.

The growth of competition and the pressure on spending will raise more and more questions about the burdens carried by colleges. As the incumbent providers, they have legacy costs built up over decades of operation. These costs include pension provision for an ageing workforce, refurbishment of their inherited buildings and a large regulatory structure. A more competitive world will see some colleges looking for ways to get rid of these costs. This links to another prediction. Colleges will look more and more like companies. Social enterprises, perhaps, but enterprises that are increasingly subject to company, consumer and competition law.

The future never looks like the past but always starts from somewhere. Financially, colleges have done well in the last decade on most measures one chooses to look at. Colleges have doubled their income from £3 billion to more than £6 billion, while continuing to make a sector-wide surplus and to invest in their future. Over ten years, colleges have spent about £4 billion on new buildings, equipment and technology. Individual colleges remain vulnerable to events and a number of colleges have been taken over by their neighbours.

The college sector as a whole is vulnerable because of its increased dependence on government funding and continued reliance on permanent staff costs, but college financial management has improved as part of a college-wide improvement in management performance. This is a sector that has delivered government targets, raised success rates, dealt quickly with poor performance when this is identified by inspectors and maintained a high level of student satisfaction.

The financial outlook for colleges will be challenging for the reasons set out in this book. Pressures to spend more on staff and other services will continue at a time when government spending will not rise. Colleges will need to perform even better to survive and thrive. Some institutions will fall by the wayside. One certain conclusion about the future is that the skills of financial management will be even more important in the next ten years than they have in the past ten. If you don't look after the money, don't expect it to look after you.

Notes

Chapter 1: The business of colleges

Financial figures on the college sector derive from College Accounts, available from the Learning and Skills Council, Coventry, England (www.lsc.gov.uk).

Financial figures on the Learning and Skills Council taken from *LSC Annual Report and Accounts 2005–6* and 'Raising our game: Our Annual Statement of Priorities for 2006–7' (LSC 2006). Both available from the Learning and Skills Council (www.lsc.gov.uk).

Figures on participation of 16 to 18 year olds in education and training derive from Department for Education and Skills statistical publications (www.dfes.gov. uk/rsgateway).

Various Department for Education and Skills documents cited include the skills strategy '21st century skills. Realising the Potential' Cm 5810 (DfES 2003), the White Paper '14–19 education and skills' Cm 6476 (DfES 2005) and the White Paper 'Further Education. Raising Skills, Improving Life Chances' Cm 6768 (DfES 2006). All available from www.dfes.gov.uk.

The further education review 'Realising the Potential: a review of the future role of further education colleges' (DfES 2005) written by Sir Andrew Foster is available from the Department for Education and Skills (www.dfes.gov.uk/further education/fereview).

Vince Hall, *Further Education in the United Kingdom* (1994), contains the Poland analogy.

Chapter 2: Financial management in colleges

The legal framework within which colleges operate is summarized in the LSC publication *Working Together for Success. A Handbook of Good Practice in LSC/College relationships* (LSC 2006).

More detailed information is available in training materials for college governers at www.ggpg.org.uk.

The Further and Higher Education Act 1992 which incorporated colleges is available from the Stationery Office (www.opsi.gov.uk/acts).

Some of the history around college developments in the 1990s is covered in A. Smithers and P. Robinson, *Further Education Re-formed (New Millenium)* (1999).

Learning and Skills Council funding guidance and financial memoranda with colleges are available from the Learning and Skills Council, Coventry, England (www.lsc.gov.uk).

Information on how the Learning and Skills Council assesses college financial health is set out in its annual guidance, *Financial Planning Handbook 2006 to 2009* (LSC 2006).

Chapter 3: Government funding

The Learning and Skills Council funding system changes constantly. For latest details, contact the Learning and Skills Council, Coventry, England (www.lsc.gov.uk/providers/funding-policy).

The Train To Gain scheme is explained at the Learning and Skills Council website (www.traintogain.gov.uk).

The Bureaucracy Task Force report 'Trust in the Future' (DfES 2002), which prompted reforms of the Learning and Skills Council funding approach, is available from the Department for Education and Skills (www.successforall.gov.uk).

The Learning and Skills Council 'Agenda for Change' (LSC 2005) is available from the Learning and Skills Council, Coventry, England (www.lsc.gov.uk).

The Audit Commission publication *Obtaining Better Value from Further Education* (1985) is now out of print.

The Further Education Funding Council publication *Funding Learning* (FEFC 1992) is now out of print.

There are no published accounts of the budget negotiations in January/February 1997 and May/June 2005 but the *Times Education Supplement* for these dates has a contemporary record of events.

Some information on the events at Halton and Bilston College is available from successive Public Accounts Committee hearings in May 1999 and March 2001 (www.parliament.uk/business/committees). These enquiries followed the National Audit Office report 'Investigations of alleged irregularities at Halton College' (NAO 1999) and a report by the former chief inspector Terry Melia, 'Bilston Community College: Report of an enquiry into its future' (FEFC 1999).

Successive Treasury spending reviews are available from HM Treasury, London (www.hm-treasury.gov.uk/spending_review).

Chapter 4: Fees, contracts and other income

Two government publications on fees, written primarily by Adrian Perry OBE, are 'Talking about Fees' (LSC 2004) and 'Fee Income: A Good Practice Guide' (DfES 2005).

The development of government policy on college fees can be traced in successive documents: 'Skills Strategy' (DfES 2003), 'Investing in Fees, Funding and Learner Support' (LSC 2004), 'Priorities for Success' (LSC 2005) and 'Further Education White Paper: Raising Skills, Improving Life Chances' (DfES 2006).

The government's higher education reforms were set out in the higher education White Paper 'The future of higher education' Cm 5735 (DfES 2003).

The Higher Education Funding Council for England explains its funding system in 'Funding higher education: how HEFCE allocates its funds' (HEFCE 2006/17).

The Prime Minister's initiative on international education is summarized in a strategy brief published in April 2006, available on the British Council website (www.britishcouncil.org).

Chapter 5: People, supplies and services

Information on the further education workforce available in the technical annex to the Further Education White Paper (www.dfes.gov.uk).

The Department for Education publication 'Managing Colleges Efficiently' (DES 1989) and Further Education Staff College publication 'Managing Resources in Further Education' (FESC 1990) are now out of print.

Information on sale of Ben Johnson Hill Associates to Tribal Group from *Tribal Group Report and Accounts 2000–1* (www.tribalgroup. gov.uk)

The Financial Reporting Standard FRS17 available from the Financial Reporting Council (www.frc.org.uk/asb/publications).

An unpublished paper on pensions in colleges available from the Association of Colleges (www.aoc.co.uk./funding).

College purchasing and procurement activities are summarized in the National Audit Office report 'Improving procurement in further education', available from the National Audit Office, London (www.nao.gov.uk).

An unpublished paper on VAT in colleges available from the Association of Colleges (www.aoc.co.uk./funding).

The Learning and Skills Development Agency guidance on VAT in further education published in 1999 is now out of print.

Chapter 6: Investment, IT and buildings

The Learning and Skills Council capital funding system changes constantly. For latest details, see the Capital Handbook available from the Learning and Skills Council, Coventry, England (www.lsc.gov.uk).

The LSC system for driving forward and funding capital projects was developed by its predecessor organization, the Further Education Funding Council. The development of the FEFC system is summarized in A. Smithers and P. Robinson, *Further Education Re-formed (New Millenium)*.

Association of Colleges' evidence to the Education and Skills Select Committee on college capital funding summarizes the position in 2006. Available from www.parliament.gov.uk.

The project to develop a unique learner number is set out in the LSC website on Managing Information Across Partners (www.miap.gov.uk).

British Education Communications and Technology Agency report 'ICT and e-learning in further education' (BECTA 2005) summarizes the state of IT in colleges.

Chapter 7: Risk, regulation and audit

Learning and Skills Council 'Audit Code of Practice', LSC circular 04–07 (LSC 2004).

Index